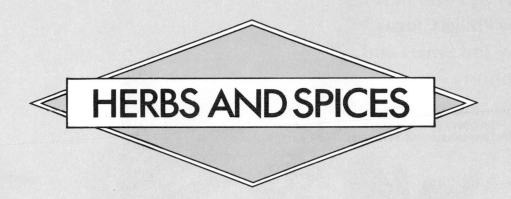

# HERBS AND SPICES

**Compiled by Judith Ferguson**
**Tested and Prepared by Jacqueline Bellefontaine**
**Photography by Peter Barry**
**Designed by Philip Clucas**
**Produced by Ted Smart and**
**David Gibbon**

Recipes for Marjoram Potatoes and Onions,
Sunshine Carrots, and Spiced Cauliflower
reproduced by kind permission of Schwartz
Spices Ltd.

CLB 1506
© 1987 Colour Library Books Ltd., Guildford,
    Surrey, England.
Text filmsetting by Focus Photoset Ltd., London, England.
Printed and bound in Barcelona, Spain by Cronion, S.A.
All rights reserved.
ISBN 0 86283 412 0

# COOKING WITH
# HERBS AND SPICES

COLOUR LIBRARY BOOKS

# CONTENTS

Soups *page 8*  Rice, Pasta, Cheese and Eggs *page 40*

Meat, Poultry and Game *page 13*  Vegetables, Salads, Oils and Vinegars *page 46*

Fish and Seafood *page 32*  Desserts, Preserves and Baking *page 54*

Index *page 64*

Herbs and spices are the heart and soul of cooking: they give food inspiration, colour and character. Vary the herbs and spices and you will give a dish individuality and make it your own. Whatever herbs and spices you choose, the following simple guidelines should prove helpful:

• Use two or three times more fresh herbs than dried.
• Crush dried herbs before using, to bring out their flavour.
• Store fresh herbs in water in the refrigerator or freeze them.
• Buy dried herbs in small amounts and keep them in airtight containers out of direct sunlight.
• Spices keep longer if bought in whole form to be ground as needed. Use a mortar and pestle, peppermill or special grinder.

• Buy pre-ground spices in small amounts and keep in airtight containers, out of direct sunlight.
• To bring out their full flavour and avoid a harsh taste, cook spices before adding any liquid to them.

The following list will acquaint you with the herbs and spices used in the recipes in this book, but the best way to learn is to experiment and taste for yourself.

**Allspice** – Whole berries or in ground form, with the taste of nutmeg, cloves and cinnamon combined. Use in pâtés, pickles, stews and curries, marinades for meat, poultry and fish, with cheese and baking and in puddings/desserts.

**Basil** – Fresh or dried leaves with a mild liquorice taste. The herb is native to Italy, France and Egypt, but grows easily elsewhere. Especially good with tomatoes and garlic. Use in all savoury Italian dishes, as well as in stews and with chicken, fish, seafood, cheese, eggs and sauces, pasta and pizza. Use raw in salads.

**Bay leaf** – Leaf of the sweet laurel tree. Native to southern Europe, but can easily be grown as an evergreen in home gardens anywhere. One of the ingredients of the classic bouquet garni. Use in stews and curries, soups and sauces, marinades for meat, poultry and fish, and also in poaching liquids for poultry and fish. Gives interesting taste to pickles and preserves. Remove before serving.

**Bergamot** – Fresh herb native to North America and Europe. Use fresh with meats, poultry and game. Plant has vivid red flowers that can be used as a tea.

**Cardamom** – Whole pods or ground spice with a sweet, lemony taste. Native to India, Ceylon and Guatemala. Whole pods can be green, brown, black or white. White cardamom is bleached and does not have as much flavour. Crush pods slightly before use to release more flavour, or use only the seeds inside. Ground cardamom is usually expensive. Use in curries and lamb dishes, with rice and in puddings/desserts.

**Celery seed** – Small brown seeds that are sometimes ground and mixed with salt for celery salt. Native to India, Turkey and Egypt. Use in pickles, with eggs and cheese, with rice and pasta, with vegetables and in salad dressings.

**Chervil** – A fresh herb with delicate flavour and fragile leaves. use in soups, salads and egg dishes.

**Chilies** – Fresh or dried, whole or crushed. Native to Central and South America, India and the Far East. Available fresh, red or green. Green chilies are the hotter of the two and the seeds are the hottest part. Mild red varieties are ground for paprika; hot for cayenne pepper. Use sparingly in meat dishes such as curries and chili con carne, and with chicken, fish, eggs, cheese, rice and pasta. Always wash hands well after handling.

**Chives** – Slender green herb with an onion taste. Originally from Denmark, but now grown in many countries. Good in any savoury dish and in salads and dressings. Use as an attractive garnish.

**Cinnamon** – Stick or ground spice from Ceylon and the Seychelle Islands with a sweet, strong taste. Use with meat and poultry, with curries and stews. Most frequent use is in desserts and puddings. Use whole sticks in pickling and preserving, and with poached fruit. Remove stick before serving. Rinsed and dried, sticks can be reused several times.

**Cloves** – Whole or ground spice from Zanzibar and Madagascar, with very strong, aromatic taste. Use with all meat, especially ham and pork, with chicken and in fish dishes such as marinated herring, in curries, sauces and pilau rice.

Most frequently used in sweet dishes and baked goods and in pickles and preserves.

**Coriander** – Spice is in seed or ground form and has a sweet, orange flavour. Leaves are used as a herb and look like flat Italian parsley, but have a very strong taste. Native to Central and South America, the Mediterranean, France, Morocco and Rumania. Also cultivated in India and Indonesia. Use in seed or ground form in stews and curries, rice, pilaffs, with chicken, cheese and eggs. Also used in sweet dishes. If using seeds, crush slightly to release more flavour. Use in leaf form like any herb, but especially in curries or Moroccan stews. Finely chopped leaves are the prominent flavour in Mexican salsas.

**Cumin** – Seed or ground spice. Very pungent and aromatic. Origin was Mediterranean, but also native to the Middle East, India and Turkey. Use in curries, Mexican dishes, marinades, chutneys, with cheese and egg dishes and grilled/broiled meats, such as kebabs.

**Curry powder** – Mixture of several ground spices such as turmeric, cumin, coriander, fenugreek, cayenne pepper and dehydrated ground garlic. Convenient, but not as flavourful as using individual spices. In addition to curries, use in chutneys, salad dressings and egg and cheese dishes.

**Dill** – Seed or fresh and dried weed. Native to Europe and the United States. Seed has a flavour similar to caraway or anise. Especially good with fish, eggs and cheese. Also use in baking, in pickles, with vegetables and in salad dressings. Fresh dill weed makes an attractive garnish.

**Fennel** – Seed, or fresh tops or weed with a mild liquorice taste. Native to Europe and India. Green tops of the Florentine fennel bulb can be used as a herb. Seeds are usually pale green. Use in Italian dishes, in curries, in sausage meat. Especially good with fish.

**Fenugreek** – Seed or ground spice. One of the ingredients in curry powder. Native to Europe, Morocco and India. Has a very strong, slightly bitter taste. Mostly used in curries.

**Garlic** – Fresh bulbs or dried powder, granules or salt. Pungent and highly aromatic. Native to southern Europe and countries with warm climates. Essential in curries and Mediterranean dishes. Use in chutneys, with eggs and cheese, rice, pasta and shellfish. Fresh garlic is the best form to use, however, 1.25ml/¼ tsp garlic powder or granules is equal to 1 clove fresh garlic.

**Ginger** – Fresh root or ground. Native to Indonesia, India, Nigeria. Hot, peppery taste with slight sweetness. Peel and grate, chop or slice the fresh root. Use in curries and Oriental dishes. Especially good with pork, ham and chicken. Use in preserves and desserts/puddings.

**Herbs de Provence** – Dried mixture of thyme, basil, savory, fennel and lavender flowers. Use with vegetables, all meats and fish. In sauces and stews with a Mediterranean influence.

**Juniper berries** – Fruit of an evergreen. Native of Europe. Use with meat, poultry, game and cabbage. Also add to pâtés.

**Lemon grass** – Native to Thailand and the Far East. Peel the outer layers and chop the core. Use in Indonesian and Oriental cooking.

**Majoram** – Fresh or dried herb. Asian and European origin. Similar taste to oregano. Use in all savoury dishes. Young leaves can be used whole as a garnish or raw in salads.

**Mint** – Fresh or dried herb. Very fragrant and sweet in its many varieties. Grown in most countries. Especially good with lamb. Use with carrots, cucumbers, peas and new potatoes. Good in fruit desserts. Fresh is preferable to dried.

**Nutmeg** – Whole berries or pre-grated spice. Native to Indonesia and West Indies. Sweet, aromatic and slightly nutty taste. Mace is the outer coating of the berry and is also available whole or ground. Use sparingly in stews and sauces (especially cheese). Good in curries and with pork and veal. Generally reserved for puddings/desserts and baking.

**Oregano** – Fresh or dried (most common). Strong and pungent. Use in Italian and Spanish cooking. Good with all meats, rice, pasta and egg dishes. Essential on pizza.

**Paprika** – Ground. Native to Hungary and Spain. Use with all meats and poultry. Add to cheese sauce and scrambled eggs. Essential in goulash and many eastern European dishes. Sprinkle onto casseroles, vegetables or fish as a garnish.

**Parsley** – Fresh or dried herb. Grown in all countries with a temperate climate. Use in stuffings, in all meat, poultry and fish dishes, sauces of all kinds, salad dressings. Use chopped or whole in salads, and whole as a garnish. Flat-leaved variety has more flavour than curly-leaved. Fresh is easily available and much better than dried.

**Peppercorns** – Black, white, green and pink. Native to India, Brazil, Ceylon and Malaysia. Use black and white peppercorns, ground as a basic seasoning. Crush the black or green peppercorns roughly for steak au poivre. Add whole to marinades or poaching liquid. Green peppercorns are fresh, unripe berries. Black are ripened and dried. White are ripened, soaked and skinned. Pink are usually preserved in vinegar. Use in all meat, poultry and fish dishes. With cheese and eggs, vegetables, rice and pasta.

**Poppy seeds** – Small black or white seeds. Native to Europe. Use in pasta and rice dishes, salad dressings and in desserts/ puddings and baked goods.

**Rosemary** – Fragrant fresh or dried herb. Native to Europe. Grows to a large evergreen shrub. Good with all meats, poultry and vegetables.

**Saffron** – Strands or powder from the stigmas of crocus flowers. Native to Italy, Spain and Portugal. Strands are expensive and powder less so, however, not much is needed to give a golden yellow colour to rice dishes like risotto and paella. Also used in delicate seafood sauces and baked goods.

**Sage** – Fresh or dried herb. Native to Europe. Good with pork, poultry and game. Ingredient in stuffings. Also used with cheese and eggs. Flavour is very strong; use sparingly.

**Savory** – Fresh or dried herb. Native to Europe. Summer and winter varieties. Use with meats, poultry, fish, eggs and fruit. Good in soups and salads.

**Tarragon** – Fresh or dried herb. French tarragon has a slight anise flavour. Russian tarragon looks the same but has less flavour. Was native to Siberia, but cultivated in France and Yugoslavia. Use with chicken, fish, eggs, game and vegetables. Classic ingredient in Bernaise sauce. Also use in vinegar and for salad dressings.

**Thyme** – Fresh or dried herb. Native to Europe and all temperate climates. Small, dark green leaves with pungent aroma. Use with all meat, poultry, game, fish dishes and vegetables. Add to rice and pasta, sauces, soups and stuffings.

**Turmeric** – Ground spice. Native to India, the Caribbean, Middle East, Africa, Ceylon. Gives curry powder its yellow colour. Use in rice dishes and with seafood. Can be used as a saffron substitute.

# HERBS AND SPICES

# SOUPS

## Chili with Three Beans

**PREPARATION TIME:** 30 minutes

**COOKING TIME:** 50 minutes - 1 hour

**SERVES:** 4-6 people

90ml/3 tbsps oil
2 medium onions, chopped roughly
1 clove garlic, crushed
15ml/1 tbsp cumin
10ml/2 tsps paprika
1 red or green chili pepper, seeded and
    chopped (use less if desired)
675g/1½ lbs minced/ground beef
790g/1¾ lbs canned tomatoes
    (approximately)
90g/3oz tomato purée/paste
5ml/1 tsp oregano
1 bay leaf
140ml/¼ pint/½ cup beer
120g/4oz/½ cup each canned red kidney
    beans, chickpeas, white kidney beans/
    pinto, drained
Salt and pepper

**GARNISH**
1 avocado, cubed
140ml/¼ pint/½ cup sour cream
Grated cheese
Chopped black olives
Corn chips or tortilla chips, roughly
    broken
Chopped fresh tomatoes
Chopped spring/green onions

Heat oil in a large, heavy-based
saucepan. Add onion and cook
slowly until transparent. Add garlic,
cumin, paprika and chili pepper and
cook for 1 minute. Add the meat and
cook until lightly browned, breaking
up large pieces with a fork. Add the
tomatoes and their juice, tomato
purée/paste, oregano, bay leaf, beer,
salt and pepper. Bring to the boil,
cover and simmer for 50 minutes to

1 hour. Check the level of liquid
several times during cooking and add
water if the chili seems to be drying
out. During the last 15 minutes of
cooking add the drained beans. Chili
can be prepared in advance and
reheated. Serve with a choice of
garnishes.

## Carrot and Basil Soup

**PREPARATION TIME:** 25 minutes

**COOKING TIME:** 22-27 minutes

**SERVES:** 4 people

45g/3 tbsps butter or margarine
2 shallots, finely chopped
6 carrots, peeled and diced
2 large potatoes, peeled and diced
1150ml/2 pints/4 cups chicken or
    vegetable stock
570ml/1 pint/2 cups water
30ml/2 tbsps chopped basil
1 bay leaf
Pinch nutmeg
Juice of ½ lemon
Salt and pepper
140ml/¼ pint/½ cup cream

**GARNISH**
Fresh basil leaves

Melt the butter or margarine in a
heavy-based pan and cook the
shallots over a gentle heat to soften.
Add the carrots and potatoes and
cook for 2 minutes, stirring
occasionally. Add the stock, water,
basil, bay leaf, nutmeg, lemon juice,
salt and pepper and cook 20-25
minutes. When the vegetables are
tender remove the bay leaf and allow
the soup to cool slightly. Purée in a
food processor or blender and add
the cream. Reheat gently and garnish
with the fresh basil leaves.

## Tomato and Tarragon Soup

**PREPARATION TIME:** 25 minutes

**COOKING TIME:** 20 minutes

**SERVES:** 4 people

60g/4 tbsps butter or margarine
1 onion, chopped
1 stick celery, thinly sliced
1 carrot, thinly sliced
5 tomatoes, roughly chopped
45ml/3 tbsps tomato purée/paste
850ml/1½ pints/3 cups vegetable stock
    or tomato juice
30ml/2 tbsps chopped fresh tarragon
1 bay leaf
Salt and pepper
60ml/4 tbsps red wine
30ml/2 tbsps cornflour/cornstarch
Pinch sugar

**GARNISH**
Finely chopped celery

Melt the butter or margarine and
cook the onion, celery and carrot
slowly until soft. Add the tomatoes,
tomato purée/paste, stock or tomato
juice, tarragon, bay leaf and salt and
pepper. Cover and simmer for 20
minutes. Remove the bay leaf and
purée the soup in a food processor or
blender. Strain out the seeds and
tomato skins through a fine sieve.
Mix the wine and cornflour/
cornstarch together and add some of
the hot soup. Return the soup to the

**Facing page: Tomato and Tarragon
Soup (top), and Carrot and Basil
Soup (bottom).**

## Asparagus and Chervil Soup

**PREPARATION TIME:** 25 minutes

**COOKING TIME:** 22-27 minutes

**SERVES:** 4 people

*60g/4 tbsps butter or margarine*
*2 shallots, finely chopped*
*225g/8oz fresh or frozen asparagus*
*340g/12oz potatoes, peeled*
*1 litre/1¾ pints/3½ cups chicken or*
*    vegetable stock*
*30g/1oz/¾ cup chopped chervil*
*Juice of ½ lemon*
*Salt and pepper*
*60ml/4 tbsps cream*

**GARNISH**
*Whole sprigs chervil*

Melt the butter or margarine in a heavy-based saucepan and soften the shallots over a gentle heat. Trim thick ends of asparagus and discard. Chop the spears into small pieces. Slice the potatoes and add the vegetables to the shallots. Cook gently for 2 minutes, stirring occasionally. Add the stock, chervil, lemon juice, salt and pepper. Cover and simmer 20-25 minutes or until the ingredients are tender. Cool slightly and purée in a food processor or blender. Stir in the cream and reheat gently. Pour into soup bowls and decorate with whole chervil leaves.

rinsed out pan and stir in the cornflour/cornstarch mixture. Bring the soup back to the boil and cook rapidly until the cornflour/cornstarch thickens. Add a pinch of sugar if necessary to bring out the tomato flavour. Serve garnished with chopped celery.

## Pea Soup with Mint

**PREPARATION TIME:** 35 minutes

**COOKING TIME:** 30 minutes

**SERVES:** 4 people

*60g/4 tbsps butter or margarine*
*2 shallots, finely chopped*
*900g/2lbs fresh shelled peas or frozen*
*    peas*
*10ml/2 tsps sugar*
*30ml/2 tbsps chopped mint*
*850ml/1½ pints/3 cups chicken or*
*    vegetable stock*
*Salt and pepper*
*60ml/4 tbsps double/heavy cream*

**GARNISH**
*Small mint leaves*

Melt butter or margarine in a large, heavy saucepan. Add shallots and cook gently until softened but not brown. Add peas and cook, stirring often, for 10 minutes. Add sugar, mint and pour on the stock. Add salt and pepper and simmer for 20 minutes, or until peas are very tender. Cool slightly and then purée in a food processor or blender. Strain into the rinsed out pan and add cream. Reheat gently and garnish with a few small whole mint leaves to serve.

## Borscht

**PREPARATION TIME:** 25 minutes

**COOKING TIME:** 35-45 minutes

**SERVES:** 4-6 people

*1150ml/2 pints/4 cups beef stock*
*2 potatoes, peeled and thinly sliced*
*1 onion, finely chopped*
*¼ head/1 cup red cabbage, shredded*
*1 bay leaf*
*Salt and pepper*

**This page: Pea Soup with Mint (top), and Asparagus and Chervil Soup (bottom). Facing page: Chili with Three Beans.**

2 large beets/beetroot or 3 small ones,
   peeled and grated
60ml/4 tbsps lemon juice
15ml/1 tbsp sugar (optional)

**GARNISH**
1 bunch chives, snipped

Combine stock, potatoes, onion,
cabbage, bay leaf, salt and pepper in a
large, deep saucepan. Bring to the
boil and then simmer until the
potatoes and cabbage are soft, about
20-25 minutes. Add beets/beetroot
and cook a further 15-20 minutes or
until all the vegetables are very soft.
Allow to cool slightly, remove the
bay leaf and purée in a food
processor or blender until smooth.
Add lemon juice to taste and a pinch
of sugar if desired. Before serving
sprinkle the soup generously with
chives. May be accompanied by sour
cream.

**This page: Borscht. Facing page:
Veal with Sorrel and Cheese
Filling (top), and Veal with
Mushrooms and Herbs (bottom).**

# MEAT, POULTRY AND GAME

## Veal with Mushrooms and Herbs

**PREPARATION TIME:** 25 minutes

**COOKING TIME:** 21-26 minutes

**SERVES:** 4 people

45g/3 tbsps butter or margarine
4 or 8 veal escalopes, depending on size
2 shallots, finely chopped
225g/8oz mushrooms, sliced or left whole
   if small
30ml/2 tbsps flour
140ml/¼ pint/½ cup stock
30ml/2 tbsps chopped fresh thyme, or
   tarragon and parsley mixed
30ml/2 tbsps sherry
180ml/6 fl oz/¾ cup milk
Salt and pepper
15ml/1 tbsp lemon juice

Melt butter or margarine in a sauté pan. When foaming, add the veal and brown 2 minutes per side. It may be necessary to brown the meat in several batches. Remove the meat and add the shallots and cook 2 minutes without browning. Add the mushrooms and cook a further 2 minutes, stirring often. Stir in the flour and cook 1 minute. Add the stock, herbs and sherry. Stir well and bring the mixture to the boil. Return the meat to the pan, cover and cook gently 10-15 minutes. When the veal is tender remove it and the mushrooms to a serving dish and keep warm. Add the milk to the pan, season and stir well. Increase the heat and allow the sauce to boil about 5 minutes to reduce. Add the lemon juice. Cover the veal escalopes and the mushrooms with the sauce before serving. Additional chopped parsley may be used to garnish if desired.

## Veal with Sorrel and Cheese Filling

**PREPARATION TIME:** 25 minutes

**COOKING TIME:** 1-1½ hours

**OVEN TEMPERATURE:** 325°F/ 150°C/Gas Mark 3

**SERVES:** 6 people

900g/2lbs rolled joint of veal
Seasoned flour

*1 egg, beaten*
*120g/4oz/1 cup dried breadcrumbs*
*45ml/3 tbsps butter or margarine, melted*

**FILLING**
*1 package garlic cheese*
*120g/4oz sorrel (substitute spinach,*
    *cooked and chopped)*
*10ml/2 tsps fresh oregano or 5ml/1 tsp*
    *dried*
*60g/2oz/¼ cup chopped walnuts*
*Pinch salt and pepper*

Unroll the veal and trim off some of the fat from the outside. Mix the filling ingredients together and spread over the meat. Roll up and sew the ends together. Dredge the veal roll with flour. Brush with beaten egg and coat with breadcrumbs. Place on a baking sheet and roast in the oven until the meat is well done, basting several times with the melted butter or margarine. Allow to stand 10 minutes before slicing to serve. Serve cold with salad, or hot with vegetables.

## Fried Pheasant with Chestnuts and Tarragon

| | |
|---|---|
| **PREPARATION TIME:** | 15 minutes |
| **COOKING TIME:** | 20-30 minutes |
| **SERVES:** | 4-6 people |

*2 prepared pheasants*
*90g/3oz/⅔ cup flour, seasoned with salt*
    *and pepper and a pinch of paprika*
*60ml/4 tbsps oil*
*60g/4 tbsps butter or margarine*
*140ml/¼ pint/½ cup white wine*
*140ml/¼ pint/½ cup stock*
*430ml/¾ pint/1½ cups double/heavy*
    *cream*
*30ml/2 tbsps chopped tarragon*
*1 small can peeled chestnuts, drained and*
    *roughly broken*
*Salt and pepper*

Cut the pheasants into quarters and trim off the wing and leg ends. Dredge in the flour. Heat the oil in a large frying pan and drop in the butter. When the fat is hot, add the pheasant pieces in one layer. Brown pieces on both sides over high heat. Reduce the heat and add the wine

**This page: Chicken Stew Niçoise. Facing page: Fried Pheasant with Chestnuts and Tarragon (top), and Devilled birds in Pasta Nest (bottom).**

and stock. Cover the pan and cook for 5 minutes over moderate heat. Uncover, and simmer about 20 minutes or until tender. Breast pieces will cook more quickly, so remove them to a plate and keep warm while cooking the remaining pheasant. Remove all the pheasant from the pan when tender, and skim off all but 15ml/1 tbsp of the fat, leaving the browned juices. Add the cream and scrape the pan to deglaze. Add the tarragon and bring the cream to the boil, stirring constantly. Allow to reduce by about half. Stir in the chestnuts and cook them briefly to heat through. Season to taste with salt and pepper and serve with the pheasant.

## Devilled Birds in Pasta Nests

| | |
|---|---|
| **PREPARATION TIME:** | 25 minutes |
| **COOKING TIME:** | 40 minutes |
| **OVEN TEMPERATURE:** | 350°F/180°C/Gas Mark 4 |
| **SERVES:** | 4 people |

*4 poussins/Cornish game hens*
*5ml/1 tsp salt*
*5ml/1 tsp paprika*
*5ml/1 tsp ground mustard*
*5ml/1 tsp ground ginger*
*2.5ml/½ tsp ground turmeric*
*1.25ml/¼ tsp ground allspice*
*60g/4 tbsps butter or margarine*
*30ml/2 tbsps chili sauce or tomato relish*
*15ml/1 tbsp mango chutney or plum*
    *sauce*
*15ml/1 tbsp brown sauce/steak sauce*
*15ml/1 tbsp Worcestershire sauce*
*15ml/1 tbsp soy sauce*

*Dash tabasco*
*60ml/4 tbsps chicken stock*

**TO SERVE**
*45ml/3 tbsps butter*
*450g/1lb cooked thin plain and spinach*
*  noodles*
*60ml/2 tbsps chopped parsley*

Tie the legs of each poussin together and tuck under the wing tips. Mix the salt and spices together and rub all sides of the poussins. Leave refrigerated for 1 hour. Place poussins in a roasting pan. Melt the butter and brush some over all sides of the poussins. Cook in a moderate oven for 20 minutes. Brush twice with butter while cooking. Mix the remaining butter with all the sauce ingredients except the stock, and heat gently. Brush each bird with some of the sauce and cook a further 20 minutes, brushing twice with the sauce mixture until the skin is brown and crisp. Melt the butter for the pasta and add the noodles and parsley to the pan. Toss over a moderate heat until hot. Arrange the noodles over the bottom of the serving dish and put the birds on top. Reheat the sauce, adding the stock. Allow the sauce to boil for 1 minute and spoon over the birds.

## Chicken Stew Niçoise

**PREPARATION TIME:** 25 minutes

**COOKING TIME:** 40 minutes-1 hour

**SERVES:** 4-6 people

*30ml/4 tbsps olive oil*
*1.5kg/3lbs chicken, cut into 8 pieces*
*6 small onions or shallots, peeled*
*2 cloves garlic, minced*
*900g/2lbs fresh tomatoes, peeled, seeded and chopped, or the same quantity of canned tomatoes, drained and broken up.*
*180ml/6 fl oz/⅓ cup white wine*
*5ml/1 tsp chopped fresh marjoram*
*Bouquet garni (sprigs thyme, 1 bay leaf, 3 parsley stalks)*
*120g/4oz/1 cup pitted black olives*
*Lemon juice*
*Salt and pepper*

Heat half the oil in a large sauté pan or heat-proof casserole. Add the chicken, skin side down, in one layer. Cook over moderate heat until golden brown on both sides, turning once. Transfer chicken to a plate and add the remaining oil to the pan if necessary. Add the onions and cook, turning often to brown evenly. Add garlic and cook 1 minute. Add tomatoes, wine and marjoram. Tie the bouquet garni ingredients with string and add along with the salt and pepper. Bring the liquid to the boil and return the chicken to the pan. Cover and simmer for 20 minutes. Uncover the pan and continue to simmer for another 15-20 minutes or until the chicken is tender. Remove chicken breasts earlier if they cook before the rest of the chicken. When all the chicken is cooked, remove it and the onions to a serving dish. Remove the bouquet garni and add the olives to the sauce. Cook the sauce rapidly to reduce it, stirring constantly, about 5 minutes. Add lemon juice if desired and pour over the chicken to serve.

## Spiced Pâté with Peppercorns

**PREPARATION TIME:** 20 minutes

**COOKING TIME:** 1½-2 hours

**OVEN TEMPERATURE:** 350°F/180°C/Gas Mark 4

**SERVES:** 6-8 people

*120-160g/4-6oz sliced bacon/streaky bacon, rinds and bones removed*
*450g/1lb lean pork, cubed*
*450g/1lb veal, cubed*
*225g/8oz belly pork/pork fat back, cubed*
*3 shallots, finely chopped*
*125ml/¼ tsp each of ginger, mace and allspice*
*10ml/2 tsps chopped fresh or dried tarragon*
*1 egg*
*45ml/3 tbsps kirsch or brandy*
*15ml/1 tbsp green peppercorns, rinsed and drained if canned*
*Salt*

Line a loaf pan or rectangular oven-proof dish with the strips of bacon, leaving the ends overlapping the edge of the dish. Combine pork, veal, belly pork/pork fat back, shallots, spices, tarragon and salt in the bowl of a food processor. Work in short bursts until chopped. Do not overwork. Add the egg and kirsch or brandy and process until just blended together. Stir in peppercorns by hand. Press the mixture into the pan on top of the bacon and fold the ends of bacon over mixture. Cover tightly with foil and place pan or dish in a roasting pan half full of hot water. Bake in a moderate oven 1½-2 hours or until pâté shrinks from the sides of the pan and the juices run clear. Cool before weighting down the top and chilling in the refrigerator overnight or until firm enough to slice easily. Serve with French bread or toast and a salad for a light meal. Pâté can also be served as a starter/appetizer.

## Country Herb Pâté

**PREPARATION TIME:** 20 minutes

**COOKING TIME:** 1½-2 hours

**OVEN TEMPERATURE:** 350°F/180°C/Gas Mark 4

**SERVES:** 8-10 people

*225g/½ lb unsmoked bacon/salt pork, cut in small pieces*
*450g/1lb lean pork, cut in small pieces*
*450g/1lb veal shoulder, cut in small pieces*
*225g/½ lb pigs' liver/pork liver, skinned and chopped*
*2 cloves garlic, crushed*
*1 onion, finely chopped*
*60g/2oz/1 cup chopped mixed herbs such as sage, thyme, dill, tarragon and marjoram*
*60g/2oz/1 cup parsley*
*120ml/¼ tsp nutmeg*
*Salt and pepper*
*1 egg*
*90ml/3 fl oz/⅓ cup brandy*

**Facing page: Country Herb Pâté (top), and Spiced Pâté with Peppercorns (bottom).**

pattern on top of the butter and spoon over another thin layer of butter to coat the bay leaves. Chill again. If the butter layer is undisturbed the pâté will keep fresh for 3-4 days in the refrigerator. Serve with French bread and a salad as a light meal or as a starter/appetizer.

## Mediterranean Lamb with Vegetables

**PREPARATION TIME:** 30 minutes

**COOKING TIME:** 2 hours 15 minutes

**OVEN TEMPERATURE:** 350°F/ 180°C/Gas Mark 4

**SERVES:** 4-6 people

560g/1¼ lbs boneless lamb shoulder or leg or neck fillets cut in 5cm/2 inch pieces
900g/2lbs fresh tomatoes, peeled, seeded and cut into large pieces, or the same quantitiy canned tomatoes, coarsely chopped and juice reserved
1 bay leaf
1 clove garlic, minced
2 onions, cut in large pieces
340g/12oz waxy potatoes, peeled and cut in 5cm/2 inch pieces
1.25ml/¼ tsp cinnamon
Pinch ground cloves
Pinch nutmeg
Salt and pepper
60ml/4 tbsps red wine
1 aubergine/eggplant cut in 2.5cm/1 inch pieces
6 courgettes/zucchini, washed and cut into 5cm/2 inch pieces
120g/4 oz mushrooms, quartered
60ml/4 tbsps capers

Combine the lamb, tomatoes and reserved juice, bay leaf, garlic, onions, potatoes, spices, salt and pepper in a casserole. Add the wine and stir. If using fresh tomatoes, add about 280ml/½ pint/1¼ cups water. Cover and cook in a moderate oven for 15 minutes. Check the amount of liquid and add water if necessary if the stew becomes too dry. Cook a further 1 hour, uncovered, making sure the potatoes stay submerged. Add the aubergine/eggplant and cook 30 minutes. Thirty minutes before the

**GARNISH**
120g/4oz/¼ cup butter, clarified
Bay leaves
Juniper berries

If using salt pork, soak for ½ hour and drain well before cutting into small pieces. Combine pork, veal and bacon/salt pork in the bowl of a food processor. Process once or twice to chop roughly. Add liver, garlic, onion, herbs, parsley, nutmeg, salt and pepper and process again to mix and chop the liver. Add egg and brandy and process once more. Process in short bursts so that the mixture does not overwork. It should be fairly coarse textured. Press the pâté into an oven-proof loaf pan or rectangular casserole dish, approximately 1.5kg/ 3lbs size. Cover the dish tightly with

foil and place it in a roasting pan half full of hot water. Cook 1-1½ hours in a moderate oven. The pâté will shrink from the sides of the pan when cooked and juices will run clear, not pink. Allow to cool and weigh down the top of the pâté. Chill in the refrigerator overnight or until completely cold. Melt the butter in a small, heavy-based saucepan. Let the butter come up to a rapid boil. Take off the heat and allow to settle for about 30 minutes. Pour or spoon off the clear butter oil from the top and discard the sediment. Spoon a layer of clarified butter over the top of pâté, about 1.25cm (½ inch) thick, and chill again until the butter solidifies. Place the juniper berries and bay leaves in a decorative

and juice, red wine, vinegar, cinnamon and cloves in a deep saucepan. Bring to the boil and then cook, covered, for 5 minutes. Add the sugar and cook a further 5 minutes. Remove the cinnamon stick and add the slivered mango. Cut the duck into quarters and serve with the sauce. Garnish with remaining mango, sliced, or orange slices, if desired.

## Ginger and Almond Meatballs

**PREPARATION TIME:** 25 minutes

**COOKING TIME:** 25 minutes

**OVEN TEMPERATURE:** 350°F/ 180°C/Gas Mark 4

**SERVES:** 4 people

90g/3oz/¾ cup blanched almonds
450g/1lb minced/ground beef
5ml/1 tsp grated fresh ginger
1 clove garlic, crushed
½ large green pepper, seeded and finely
    chopped
30ml/2 tbsps soy sauce
Dash Szechwan chili sauce or tabasco
Salt
Oil for frying

**SAUCE**
45ml/3 tbsps soy sauce
120ml/4 fl oz/½ cup water or stock
15ml/1 tbsp rice or white wine vinegar
10ml/2 tsps honey
15ml/1 tbsp sherry
15ml/1 tbsp cornflour/cornstarch

**GARNISH**
4 spring/green onions, sliced or shredded

Toast almonds on baking sheet for 10-15 minutes, stirring often until golden brown. Allow to cool completely and chop. Mix the almonds with the meat and ginger, garlic, pepper, soy sauce, chili sauce or tabasco and salt. Form the mixture into a 3.75cm/1½ inch

end of cooking, add the remaining ingredients. Skim any fat from the surface and remove the bay leaf before serving with pasta or rice.

## Duck with Cranberries and Mangoes

**PREPARATION TIME:** 30 minutes

**COOKING TIME:** 1 hour 15 minutes

**OVEN TEMPERATURE:** 450°F/ 230°C/Gas Mark 8

**SERVES:** 4 people

1-2kg/2½ lbs duck
Oil
Salt

**SAUCE**
120g/4oz/2 cups fresh cranberries
Grated rind and juice of 2 oranges
90ml/3 fl oz/⅓ cup red wine
15ml/1 tbsp red wine vinegar
1 stick cinnamon
Pinch ground cloves
60g/2 oz/¼ cup sugar
½ mango, peeled and slivered

Prick the duck skin all over with a sharp fork or skewer. Rub oil into the skin and sprinkle over salt. Roast the duck on a rack, breast side down, for 15 minutes. Turn on one side and roast for 15 minutes. Turn onto the other side and roast for 15 minutes. Then roast breast side up for 30 minutes. Drain the fat away several times during roasting. Meanwhile, combine the cranberries, orange rind

**Facing page: Mediterranean Lamb with Vegetables. This page: Duck with Cranberries and Mangoes.**

of the chops and snip the edges to prevent curling. Combine all the remaining ingredients except the pink berries. Spread ⅓ of the butter mixture over one side of the chops. Grill/broil slowly 15-20 minutes on one side. Turn over and spread ⅓ of the butter on the other side. Grill/broil again slowly 15-20 minutes. Make a small cut on the under side of one of the chops to check for doneness. If not completely cooked grill/broil another 5 minutes. Remove the chops and keep warm. Reheat the remaining butter and add the pink berries. Pour over the chops to serve.

## Sauté Lamb with Fennel and Orange

| **PREPARATION TIME:** 30 minutes |
| **COOKING TIME:** 45 minutes |
| **SERVES:** 4 people |

60g/2 tbsps butter or margarine
675g/1½ lbs neck fillets of lamb
3 shallots, finely chopped
30g/2 tbsps flour
340ml/¾ pint/1½ cups stock
Grated rind and juice of 1 orange
30ml/2 tbsps chopped fennel tops
1 bay leaf
Salt and pepper

**GARNISH**
1 orange, peeled and sliced or segmented

Melt butter or margarine in a sauté pan. Cut lamb in 1.25cm/½ inch slices and brown on both sides quickly. Remove and keep warm. Lower the heat and cook shallots to soften. Remove shallots and add flour to the pan. Brown slowly, stirring often to prevent sticking and burning. When golden brown, pour on stock and orange juice and rind and bring to the boil to mix thoroughly. Return lamb and shallots to the pan and add the fennel tops, bay leaf, salt and pepper. Cover the pan and simmer the lamb for 40 minutes or until tender. Remove the bay leaf before serving. Scatter over orange segments or arrange orange slices around the lamb and serve with rice.

**This page: Grilled/Broiled Pork Chop with Herbs and Pink Berries. Facing page: Saute Lamb with Fennel and Orange (top), and Ginger and Almond Meatballs (bottom).**

balls. Heat the oil in a large frying pan and brown the meatballs in one layer. Cook over low to moderate heat for about 20 minutes, turning several times. Transfer to a serving dish and keep warm. Pour off most of the fat, leaving the meat juices. Add soy sauce, stock and vinegar to the pan and bring to the boil. Add the honey and stir to dissolve. Mix the sherry and cornflour/cornstarch together. Stir into the hot sauce and cook until thickened. Pour over the meatballs and sprinkle over the spring/green onions. Serve with rice.

## Grilled/Broiled Pork Chops with Herbs and Pink Berries

| **PREPARATION TIME:** 20 minutes |
| **COOKING TIME:** 30-40 minutes |
| **SERVES:** 4 people |

4 pork loin chops, 2.5cm/1 inch thick
60g/4 tbsps butter, softened
1 shallot, finely chopped
15ml/1 tbsp chopped parsley
15ml/1 tbsp chopped marjoram
15ml/1 tbsp chopped thyme
Leaves from 1 sprig rosemary
Squeeze lemon juice
15ml/1 tbsp pink berries, drained if canned

Trim some of the fat from the outside

## Ham with Spiced Raisin Sauce

**PREPARATION TIME:** 20 minutes

**COOKING TIME:** 25 minutes

**SERVES:** 4 people

30ml/2 tbsps butter or margarine
4 cooked ham slices or steaks

SAUCE
280ml/½ pint/1 cup cider
60g/2oz/½ cup raisins
1.25ml/¼ tsp nutmeg
1.25ml/¼ tsp cloves
10ml/2 tsps cornflour/cornstarch mixed
    with 30ml/2 tbsps cider
15ml/1 tbsp Calvados (optional)
Salt

GARNISH
Coriander leaves

Melt butter or margarine in a frying pan. Brown 2 ham steaks at a time on both sides. Remove the ham and keep warm. Deglaze the pan with the cider, reserving 30ml/2 tbsps to mix with cornflour/cornstarch. Add the raisins and cook about 5 minutes. Add the spices and salt and stir in the cornflour/cornstarch mixture. Bring to the boil and cook until thickened. Add Calvados to the hot sauce and pour over the ham to serve. Garnish with coriander leaves.

## Five Spice Pork

**PREPARATION TIME:** 25 minutes

**COOKING TIME:** 42 minutes

**SERVES:** 4 people

450g/1lb pork chops, boned
60ml/4 tbsps oil
1 small piece fresh ginger, peeled
5ml/1 tsp Szechwan or black peppercorns
5ml/1 tsp five spice powder
140ml/¼ pint/½ cup dry sherry
280ml/½ pint/1¼ cups light stock
60ml/4 tbsps honey
4 spring/green onions, cut in large pieces
60g/2oz bamboo shoots, shredded
1 mango, peeled and sliced

Heat the oil in a large frying pan or wok and add the ginger. Lower the chops into the hot oil and cook them quickly to brown. Remove the meat and set aside. Add peppercorns and fry 2 minutes. Add five spice powder, sherry, stock, honey and bring to the boil. Return the pork chops to the pan or wok, cover, and simmer over low heat for 40 minutes or until the pork is tender. About 4 minutes before the end of cooking time add onions, bamboo shoots and mango. Remove the ginger before serving with rice or crisp noodles

## Chicken Marrakesh with Peppers and Coriander

**PREPARATION TIME:** 30 minutes

**COOKING TIME:** 1 hour 30 minutes

**SERVES:** 4-6 people

2 red peppers, halved and seeded
1 green pepper, halved and seeded
Oil for brushing

SAUCE
15ml/1 tbsp olive oil
10ml/2 tsps paprika
1.25ml/¼ tsp cumin
Pinch cayenne pepper
2 cloves garlic, crushed
450g/1lb fresh tomatoes, peeled, seeded
    and chopped, or same quantity canned
    tomatoes, drained and broken up
45ml/3 tbsps chopped fresh coriander
45ml/3 tbsps chopped parsley
Salt

30ml/2 tbsps olive oil
1.5kg/3lbs chicken, quartered
1 large onion, sliced
1 clove garlic, crushed
Pinch sugar (optional)

GARNISH
Sliced/flaked almonds

Pre-heat grill/broiler. Flatten the peppers slightly and brush skin side with oil. Grill/broil until charred on the outside. Wrap peppers in a clean towel for 10 minutes. Unwrap and peel off the charred skin. Chop the peppers into small pieces. Meanwhile heat 15ml/1 tbsp olive oil in a heavy pan. Add the spices and garlic and cook gently for 2 minutes. Stir often and do not allow the garlic to brown. Add remaining sauce ingredients and chopped peppers and cook 15-20 minutes over moderate heat until the sauce is thick. Set aside. Use a heavy casserole large enough to accommodate the chicken in one layer. Heat 30ml/2 tbsps olive oil and add the chicken, skin side down. Cook over moderate heat until golden brown on both sides, turning once. Remove the chicken and add the onions and garlic. Cook to soften the onion, about 5 minutes, over a gentle heat. Return chicken to the casserole and pour on about 280ml/½ pint/1 cup water and bring to the boil. Cover and simmer for 30 minutes, turning the chicken occasionally. Remove the chicken and boil the remaining liquid to reduce to about 90ml/3 fl oz/⅓ cup. Add the pepper sauce and adjust the seasoning. Add a pinch of sugar if necessary to bring out the tomato flavour. Return the chicken to the casserole and cook for additional 30 minutes on gentle heat. When the chicken is tender, cut the leg joints into 2 pieces and the breast and wing joints into 2 pieces and set aside. Remove any fat from the surface of the sauce. Coat the chicken with the sauce and sprinkle with flaked/sliced almonds.

## Moroccan Chicken

**PREPARATION TIME:** 25 minutes

**COOKING TIME:** 1 hour

**SERVES:** 4-6 people

Few strands saffron
60ml/4 tbsps hot water
45ml/3 tbsps oil
1.5kg/3lbs chicken, quartered
2 onions, finely chopped
180ml/6 fl oz/¾ cup water or chicken
    stock
1 cinnamon stick
Salt and pepper
30g/2 tbsps butter or margarine
120g/4oz/1 cup blanched whole almonds

**Facing page: Five Spice Pork (top), and Ham with Spiced Raisin Sauce (bottom).**

*150g/5oz/1¼ cups dried apricots*
*30ml/2 tbsps honey*
*Nutmeg*
*Lemon juice*

Soak the saffron in the hot water in a small bowl for 20 minutes. Heat the oil in a large pan or casserole and add the chicken, skin side down, in one layer. Brown over moderate heat on both sides and remove from the pan. Add the onions, and cook until soft but not browned. Return the chicken to the pan and add the saffron water, stock or water, cinnamon stick, salt and pepper. Bring to the boil and simmer 25 minutes or until the breast pieces are cooked. Remove those to a plate and cook remaining chicken another 10 to 15 minutes or until tender. Meanwhile, melt the butter or margarine in a frying pan and cook the almonds slowly until golden brown. Drain on a paper towel. Skim any fat from the surface of the sauce and add the apricots and cook for 10 to 15 minutes or until just tender. Remove the cinnamon stick and stir in the honey, nutmeg and lemon juice and return the chicken to the pan to reheat. Serve chicken in the sauce, garnished with toasted almonds.

## Herb-Roasted Guinea Fowl with Redcurrants

**PREPARATION TIME:** 30 minutes

**COOKING TIME:** 1 hour

**OVEN TEMPERATURE:** 375°F/ 190°C/Gas Mark 5

**SERVES:** 4 people

*2 oven-ready guinea fowl*
*30g/2 tbsps softened butter*

**STUFFING**
*45g/3 tbsps butter or margarine*
*3 shallots, finely chopped*
*15ml/1 tbsp chopped parsley*
*15ml/1 tbsp chopped marjoram*
*15ml/1 tbsp chopped fresh thyme leaves*
*5ml/1 tsp chopped sage*
*5ml/1 tsp very finely chopped rosemary leaves*
*180g/6oz/1½ cups fresh breadcrumbs*
*Salt and pepper*

**This page: Moroccan Chicken (top), and Chicken Marrakesh with Peppers and Coriander. Facing page: Herb-Roasted Guinea Fowl with Redcurrants.**

**SAUCE**
*15ml/1 tbsp red wine vinegar*
*280ml/½ pint/1 cup chicken stock*
*30ml/2 tbsps arrowroot*
*225g/8oz canned or fresh redcurrants, stems removed*
*15ml/1 tbsp redcurrant jelly*

**GARNISH**
*Fresh redcurrants, if available, or fresh herbs*

First prepare the stuffing. Melt the butter or margarine in a small, heavy-based saucepan. Add the shallots and cook until softened, but not browned. Allow to cool slightly. Stir in remaining stuffing ingredients, mixing well. Loosen the skin on each guinea fowl over the breast and thighs. Divide the stuffing between the two birds and push half up under the skin of each, spreading it out as evenly as possible over the breast and thighs. Divide the remaining butter in half and spread over the outside of each bird. Close the cavity with skewers or sew with string. Tie the legs together and pat each bird into an attractive shape. Cook in a roasting pan in a preheated oven for about 1 hour, basting 2 or 3 times with the butter and pan juices. Allow to rest in a warm place for at least 5 minutes before cutting in half with poultry shears to serve. To make the sauce, skim all but 15ml/1 tbsp of fat from the roasting pan, add the vinegar to the pan and heat to reduce the vinegar slightly. Mix 30ml/ 2 tbsps of the chicken stock with the arrowroot and set aside. Add the remaining stock and redcurrants to the vinegar in the roasting pan. If using canned redcurrants, substitute the juice for part of the stock. Crush the currants with the back of a spoon. Bring the mixture to the boil and allow to boil rapidly to reduce by about one quarter. Stir in the redcurrant jelly and mix to dissolve. Stir some of the hot liquid into the arrowroot mixture and then add it to the roasting pan. Stirring constantly, bring to the boil to thicken. Add grated nutmeg, salt and pepper, and strain if desired. Coat some of the sauce over each guinea fowl and serve surrounded by fresh currants or herbs. Serve remaining sauce separately.

## Liver with Coriander, Lemon and Pine Nuts

**PREPARATION TIME:** 25 minutes

**COOKING TIME:** 5-6 minutes

**SERVES:** 4 people

45ml/3 tbsps olive oil
450g/1lb calves or lambs liver, skinned, trimmed and cut into strips
1 large onion, thinly sliced
60g/2oz/½ cup pine nuts
10ml/2 tsps ground coriander
30ml/2 tbsps lemon juice
Salt and pepper

**GARNISH**
Fresh coriander leaves
Lemon slices

Heat the oil in a large frying pan. Add the liver and fry quickly over high heat. Remove the liver and keep it warm. Add the onions and pine nuts and fry until golden. Add the coriander and cook 1-2 minutes over low heat. Return liver to the pan and

pour over the lemon juice. Season with salt and pepper and heat through for 1-2 minutes. Serve garnished with coriander and lemon slices.

## Chicken Moghlai with Coriander Chutney

**PREPARATION TIME:** 25 minutes

**COOKING TIME:** 30-40 minutes

**SERVES:** 4-6 people

60ml/4 tbsps oil
1.5kg/3lbs chicken pieces, skinned
8 cardamom pods, slightly crushed or 5ml/1 tsp ground cardamom
Small piece stick cinnamon or 2.5ml/ ½ tsp ground cinnamon
1 bay leaf
4 whole cloves
2 onions, peeled and finely chopped
1 small piece fresh ginger, peeled and grated
4 cloves garlic, crushed
30g/1oz/¼ cup ground blanched almonds
10ml/2 tsps cumin seed or ground cumin
Pinch cayenne pepper
280ml/½ pint/1 cup single/light cream
90ml/3 fl oz/⅓ cup natural yogurt
15-30ml/1-2 tbsps roasted cashews
15-30ml/1 to 2 tbsps sultanas/golden raisins
Salt

necessary. The mixture will look separated. Do not allow the sauce to boil once the yogurt has been added. Remove the bay leaf before serving with rice and coriander chutney. To prepare chutney, combine the coriander, chili pepper, lemon juice, salt, pepper and sugar in a food processor or blender and work to a paste. Heat the oil and cook the ground coriander 1 minute. Add the other ingredients and process again until well mixed.

## Chicken Cacciatore

**PREPARATION TIME:** 20 minutes

**COOKING TIME:** 1 hour 15 minutes

**SERVES:** 4-6 people

*60ml/4 tbsps olive oil*
*1.5kg/3lbs chicken pieces*
*2 onions, sliced*
*3 cloves garlic, crushed*
*225g/8oz mushrooms, quartered*
*140ml/¼ pint/½ cup red wine*
*15ml/1 tbsp wine vinegar*
*15ml/1 tbsp chopped parsley*
*10ml/2 tsps oregano, chopped fresh or*
  *crumbled dry*
*10ml/2 tsps basil, chopped fresh or*
  *crumbled dry*
*1 bay leaf*
*450g/1lb canned tomatoes*
*140ml/¼ pint/½ cup chicken stock*
*Salt and pepper*
*Pinch sugar*

**CHUTNEY**
*90g/3oz/about 2 cups fresh coriander*
  *(leaves only)*
*1 small green chili pepper, coarsely*
  *chopped*
*15ml/1 tbsp lemon juice*
*Salt and pepper*
*Pinch sugar*
*15ml/1 tbsp oil*
*2.5ml/½ tsp ground coriander*

Heat the oil for the chicken in a large sauté or frying pan. Place the chicken in the hot oil in one even layer. Fry until golden brown on both sides. Repeat until all the chicken is browned and remove the chicken to a plate. Add the cardamom, cinnamon, bay leaf and cloves to the

oil and fry for a few seconds. Add the onions and fry, stirring often, for about 4-5 minutes over moderate heat. Cook until lightly browned. Add the ginger, garlic, almonds, cumin and cayenne pepper. Cook over a moderate heat for about 2-3 minutes. Add the cream gradually, stirring constantly. Return the chicken and any of the accumulated juices to the pan. Cover the pan and simmer gently for about 30-40 minutes or until the chicken is tender, stirring occasionally. Remove the breast pieces if they cook before the rest of the chicken and keep them warm. Add the yogurt to the chicken and stir well. Add the cashews, sultanas/golden raisins and salt, if

Heat the oil in a large sauté or frying pan. When the oil is hot add the chicken pieces, skin side down, in one layer. Brown on both sides and remove to a plate. Repeat until all the chicken is browned. Add the onions and garlic to the pan and cook to brown lightly. Add the mushrooms and cook about 1 minute. Pour on the wine and vinegar and bring to the boil. Boil to reduce by about half quantity. Add the herbs, bay leaf and tomatoes with

**This page: Liver with Coriander, Lemon and Pine Nuts. Facing page: Chicken Moghlai with Coriander Chutney (top), and Chicken Cacciatore (bottom).**

their juice. Break up the tomatoes slightly. Add the chicken stock and reboil. Add salt, pepper and a pinch of sugar to taste and return chicken and accumulated juices to the pan. Cover and simmer for 1 hour, or transfer to a heat-proof casserole and cook for 1 hour in a moderate oven or until the chicken is tender. Skim the fat from the surface of the sauce if necessary. Serve with pasta or rice.

## Spinach and Chicken Terrine

**PREPARATION TIME:** 25 minutes

**COOKING TIME:** 1 hour

**SERVES:** 4-6 people

225g/8oz chicken breasts, boned and skinned
2 egg whites
120g/4oz/1 cup fresh white breadcrumbs
450g/1lb spinach, washed
45ml/3 tbsps chopped chervil, chives and tarragon, mixed
280ml/½ pint/1 cup double/heavy cream
60g/2oz/½ cup finely chopped walnuts
Nutmeg
Salt and pepper
Fromage blanc or low fat cream cheese mixed with milk to piping consistency

Mix the chicken, 1 egg white, half the breadcrumbs, salt and pepper in a food processor and purée until well mixed. Cook the spinach in the water that clings to the leaves for 3 minutes or until just wilted. Remove the chicken from the food processor and rinse the bowl. Put the spinach into the food processor with the herbs, remaining egg white and breadcrumbs, salt, pepper and nutmeg. Process until well mixed. Divide the cream in half and mix half with the chicken mixture and half with the spinach. Add the walnuts to the spinach mixture with the cream. Line a 450g/1lb loaf pan with waxed/ greaseproof paper and spread in the chicken mixture. Cover with the spinach mixture and carefully smooth out the top. Cover the pan with greased foil, sealing tightly. Place the pan in a dish of warm water and cook at 325°F/150°C/Gas Mark 3

for 1 hour or until firm. Chill overnight. Carefully lift out using the paper. Peel off the paper carefully and cut the terrine into slices. Beat the cheese until smooth and pipe lines or lattice on the top of each slice of terrine. Serve as an appetizer/starter or with a salad as a light main course.

## Chicken Liver Pâté with Coriander

**PREPARATION TIME:** 15 minutes

**COOKING TIME:** 20 minutes

**SERVES:** 4 people

450g/1lb chicken livers, trimmed
225g/8oz butter
4 shallots, finely chopped
2 cloves garlic, chopped
2.5ml/½ tsp ground coriander
10ml/2 tsps chopped parsley
Salt and pepper
10ml/2 tsps mango chutney

**GARNISH**
Coriander leaves
Clarified butter

If livers are large, cut in even-sized pieces. Melt half the butter in a sauté pan. Add the shallots, garlic, coriander and livers and cook together over moderate heat until livers are cooked through. Allow to cool completely and purée in a food processor or blender. Push through a metal sieve if a smoother pâté is desired. Add remaining butter, parsley, salt and pepper and chutney. Process again until smooth, and transfer to a serving dish. Coat with clarified butter prepared as for Country Herb Pâté. Decorate with coriander leaves. Serve with toast.

## Tunisian Beef Stew with Okra

**PREPARATION TIME:** 30 minutes

**COOKING TIME:** 2 hours 25 minutes

**SERVES:** 4-6 people

60ml/4 tbsps olive oil
900g/2lbs braising steak/chuck steak, cut into 5cm/2 inch pieces
2 onions, sliced

15ml/1 tbsp cumin
10ml/2 tsps paprika
4 cloves garlic, chopped
675g/1½ lbs fresh tomatoes, peeled, seeded and chopped, or the same quantity canned tomatoes, drained and broken up
430ml/¾ pint/1½ cups stock or water
1 bay leaf
15ml/1 tbsp chopped parsley or fresh coriander
120g/4oz okra, stems trimmed
Salt and pepper

Heat the oil in a large heavy-based saucepan or heat-proof casserole. Add the steak pieces in one layer and cook over a high heat to brown on all sides. Brown in several batches, about 6 minutes per batch. Remove the meat and lower the heat. Add the onions and cook to brown lightly and soften. Add the spices and garlic and cook 2 minutes on gentle heat. Add tomatoes, stock or water, bay leaf, parsley or coriander, salt and pepper. Bring to the boil, and then cover and simmer for 2 hours, stirring occasionally. Uncover, add the okra and simmer for 15 minutes. The okra will help to thicken the cooking liquid. Remove the bay leaf and serve with rice or couscous.

## Navarin of Lamb Printanier

**PREPARATION TIME:** 25 minutes

**COOKING TIME:** 1 hour 30 minutes

**OVEN TEMPERATURE:** 325°F/ 150°C/Gas Mark 3

**SERVES:** 4 people

30ml/2 tbsps oil
4 lamb chops
1 onion, sliced
2 cloves garlic, crushed
60g/4 tbsps flour
700ml/1¼ pints/2½ cups stock
30ml/2 tbsps tomato purée/paste

**Facing page: Spinach and Chicken Terrine (top), and Chicken Liver Pâté with Coriander (bottom).**

*1 tsp fresh rosemary leaves*
*1 tsp fresh thyme*
*675g/1½ lbs of the following vegetables:*
*  celery, cut in 5cm/2 inch pieces: small*
*  new potatoes, scrubbed, carrots, cut*
*  into thick barrel shapes, small turnips,*
*  peeled and trimmed, French/green*
*  beans, cut into 5cm/2 inch pieces,*
*  small onions or shallots, peeled,*
*  mangetout/pea pods, ends trimmed*

Heat the oil in a heat-proof casserole.
When the oil is hot, brown the chops

on all sides and remove them to a
plate and keep warm. Add the onion
and garlic. Sauté for 2-3 minutes.
Stir in the flour and allow to brown
for 1 to 2 minutes. Gradually stir in
the stock and add the tomato purée/
paste and herbs. Bring to the boil,
stirring constantly. Replace the meat,
cover and cook at 325°F/150°C/Gas
Mark 3 for 45 minutes. Add the root
vegetables such as potatoes, carrots,
celery and turnips, stir well and cover
and cook for 20-30 minutes or until

**This page: Tunisian Beef Stew
with Okra. Facing page: Navarin
of Lamb Printanier.**

meat and vegetables are tender. Add
the green vegetables such as French/
green beans and mangetout/pea pods
during the last 15 minutes of cooking.
Skim any fat from the surface of the
sauce and remove the bay leaf before
serving.

# HERBS AND SPICES

# FISH AND SEAFOOD

1.25ml/¼ tsp turmeric
½ green chili pepper, seeded and chopped
Juice of ½ a lime
140ml/¼ pint/½ cup single/light cream
Salt and pepper

Discard any mussels that are open or have cracked shells. Put mussels into a large, deep pan and sprinkle over 1 shallot. Add the bay leaf and wine. Cover the pan and bring to the boil, shaking the pan. Cook about 3 minutes or until the mussels have opened. Set aside and keep covered. Melt the butter in a saucepan and add the remaining chopped shallot. Soften for 2 minutes and add the ginger, cumin, turmeric and chili pepper. Add the lime juice and strain on the cooking liquid from the mussels. Bring to the boil, stirring occasionally and allow to boil to reduce by half. Pour on the cream and reboil to reduce slightly and thicken. Divide the mussels between 4 serving bowls and pour on the sauce. Sprinkle the parsely over each serving. Serve as a starter/appetizer, or double the quantity to serve 4 as a main course. Accompany with wholemeal French bread.

## Scallops in Saffron Sauce

**PREPARATION TIME:** 15 minutes

**COOKING TIME:** 15 minutes

**SERVES:** 4 people

16 large scallops with roe attached
140ml/¼ pint/½ cup water

**This page: Prawns/Shrimp with Red Pepper Sauce. Facing page: Mussels in Ginger-Cumin Sauce (top), and Scallops in Saffron Sauce (bottom).**

## Mussels in Ginger-Cumin Sauce

**PREPARATION TIME:** 20 minutes

**COOKING TIME:** 10 minutes

**SERVES:** 4 people

1kg/2.2lbs mussels in their shells, scraped
2 shallots, chopped
1 bay leaf
90ml/3 fl oz/⅓ cup white wine
30g/2 tbsps butter
1 small piece ginger, grated
2.5ml/½ tsp cumin

140ml/¼ pint/½ cup white wine
1 shallot, roughly chopped
Bouquet garni (1 bay leaf, 1 sprig fresh
   thyme, 3 parsley stalks)
6 black peppercorns
Pinch salt

SAUCE
Few strands saffron, soaked in 60ml/
   4 tbsps hot water
340ml/10 fl oz/1¼ cups double/heavy
   cream
45ml/3 tbsps chopped parsley
Salt and pepper

Place the scallops in a large, shallow pan with the water, wine shallot, bouquet garni and peppercorns. Cover the pan and bring the liquid almost to the boil. Take off the heat and leave covered for 10-15 minutes. The scallops should cook in the heat of the liquid. If the scallops are just firm to the touch remove them to a plate and keep warm. Strain the saffron cooking liquid into a small saucepan. Bring the liquid to the boil and allow to boil rapidly to reduce by about half. Add the saffron and the soaking liquid, double/heavy cream, chopped parsley, salt and pepper to the saucepan. Bring the sauce back to the boil and allow to bubble until the cream thickens slightly. Pour over the scallops to serve. Serve as a starter/appetizer or with rice or pasta as a light main course.
Note: Ready-made bouquets garni are available in spice sections of supermarkets and speciality shops.

## Prawns/Shrimp with Red Pepper Sauce

**PREPARATION TIME:** 20 minutes

**COOKING TIME:** 20 minutes

**SERVES:** 4 people

675g/1½ lbs uncooked, peeled king
   prawns/jumbo shrimp
140ml/¼ pint/½ cup water
140ml/¼ pint/½ cup white wine
3 black peppercorns
1 small bay leaf

SAUCE
60g/2oz butter or margarine

1 large or 2 small red peppers, seeded and
   chopped
1 to 2 red chili peppers, seeded and
   chopped
5ml/1 tsp ground coriander
60g/2oz/½ cup ground blanched
   almonds
60g/4 tbsps desiccated coconut
Juice of 1 lime
45ml/3 tbsps natural yogurt
4 spring/green onions, sliced

Place the prawns/shrimp, water, wine, peppercorns and bay leaf in a shallow pan. Bring almost to the boil and cover the pan tightly. Leave to stand for 10 minutes. Prawns/shrimp should cook in the heat of the liquid. Melt the butter or margarine in a saucepan, add the red pepper, chili pepper, and coriander. Cook slowly until the peppers are very soft. Pour into a food processor or blender and add the almonds, coconut and lime juice. Strain off the cooking liquid from the prawns/shrimp. Process until smooth. Reheat the sauce and stir in the yogurt. Pour over the prawns/shrimp. Process until smooth. Reheat the sauce and stir in the yogurt. Pour over the prawns and sprinkle on the spring/green onions. Serve with rice.

## Seviche

**PREPARATION TIME:** 20 minutes

**SERVES:** 4 people

450g/1lb cod fillets
Juice and grated rind of 2 limes
1 shallot, chopped
1 green chili pepper
5ml/1 tsp crushed coriander seeds
1 small green pepper
1 small, sweet red pepper
15ml/1 tbsp chopped parsley
15ml/1 tbsp chopped fresh coriander
4 spring/green onions, chopped
30ml/2 tbsps olive oil
Salt and pepper
1 small lettuce

Skin the cod fillets and cut into thin strips across the grain. Put into a bowl and pour over the lime juice and the rind. Add the shallot, chili pepper, crushed coriander seeds

and cover the bowl. Leave in the refrigerator for 24 hours, stirring occasionally. When ready to serve, slice the peppers and spring/green onions. Drain the fish and stir in the oil. Add the peppers and herbs and toss. Shred the lettuce and arrange on serving plates. Top with seviche to serve.

## Gravad Laks with Mustard Dill Sauce

**PREPARATION TIME:** 15 minutes, plus marinating time

**SERVES:** 6-8 people

450g/1lb filleted centre cut of salmon,
   unskinned
15ml/1 tbsp coarsely ground sea salt
12 crushed white peppercorns
30ml/2 tbsps sugar
45ml/3 tbsps chopped fresh dill
2.5ml/½ tsp crushed allspice berries
30ml/2 tbsps brandy

SAUCE
15ml/1 tbsp strong mustard, such as Dijon
15ml/1 tbsp sweet Swedish-style mustard
15ml/1 tbsp sugar
15ml/1 tbsp oil
10ml/2 tsps white wine vinegar
Salt and pepper
15ml/1 tbsps chopped fresh dill

Remove as many of the small bones as possible from the salmon. Rinse the fish and pat dry. Combine salt, peppercorns, sugar, dill and allspice and rub evenly onto each piece of salmon on the flesh side. Sprinkle the brandy over each side and press the two sides together, skin side outermost. Wrap tightly in foil. Place in a shallow dish and weight down the top of the fish. Leave for 24 to 36 hours in the refrigerator. Turn the parcels several times and weight down after each turning. Scrape off most of the dill and spices and slice the fish on a slant, across the grain, into thin slices. Discard the skin. To prepare the sauce combine the

**Facing page: Gravad Laks with Mustard Dill Sauce (top), and Seviche (bottom).**

mustard and sugar. Gradually add the oil in a thin, steady stream, whisking constantly. Add the vinegar gradually to thin slightly. Sauce should be the consistency of thick cream. Season with salt and pepper and add more sugar or vinegar if desired. Stir in the dill and serve with gravad laks.

## Poached Smoked Haddock in Herb Sauce

**PREPARATION TIME:** 10 minutes

**COOKING TIME:** 20 minutes

**SERVES:** 4 people

*8 smoked haddock fillets of even size*
*Mixture of water and milk to cover the*
*    fish*
*Bouquet garni (1 bay leaf, 1 sprig thyme,*
*    3 parsley stalks)*
*6 black peppercorns*

**SAUCE**
*45g/3 tbsps butter or margarine*
*45g/3 tbsps flour*
*280ml/½ pint/1 cup milk*
*60ml/4 tbsps fresh mixed herbs, finely*
*    chopped*
*½ small bunch watercress leaves*
*Salt and pepper*

Arrange the fish fillets skin side up in a large, shallow pan. Pour over enough water and milk mixed to cover the fish and add the bouquet garni. Cover the pan and bring the liquid almost to the boil. Leave the pan covered for 10-15 minutes to allow the fish to cook in the hot liquid. If the fillets are very thick it may be necessary to cook the fish a bit longer before leaving to stand. Melt the butter for the sauce and when foaming stir in the flour. Cook to a very pale straw colour. Pour on the milk gradually, stirring continuously. Remove the haddock to a serving dish and arrange skin side down on the plate. Strain 280ml/½ pint/1 cup of the fish cooking liquid and add to the sauce. Whisk the sauce well to blend thoroughly and add the herbs and the salt and pepper. Stirring constantly, bring the sauce to the boil and allow to boil for about 2 minutes or until

thickened. Combine with the watercress leaves in a food processor or blender and purée until the watercress leaves are finely chopped. If necessary, return to the pan to heat through. Spoon some of the sauce over the haddock fillets and serve the rest separately.

## Grilled/Broiled Herring with Dill and Mustard

**PREPARATION TIME:** 10 minutes

**COOKING TIME:** 12-15 minutes

**SERVES:** 4 people

*60ml/4 tbsps chopped fresh dill*

**This page: Red Mullet with Herbs en Papillote. Facing page: Grilled/Broiled Herring with Dill and Mustard (top), and Poached Smoked Haddock in Herb Sauce (bottom).**

*90ml/3 fl oz/⅓ cup mild Swedish*
*    mustard*
*30ml/2 tbsps lemon juice or white wine*
*4-8 fresh herring, cleaned but heads and*
*    tails left on*
*30ml/2 tbsps butter or margarine, melted*
*Salt and pepper*

**GARNISH**
*Lemon wedges*
*Whole sprigs of fresh dill*

30ml/2 tbsps coconut cream
570ml/1 pint/2 cups water
120g/4oz shrimps, peeled
120g/4oz chicory, shredded
225g/8oz Chinese leaves/cabbage,
    shredded
15ml/1 tbsp dark brown sugar
Salt
15-30ml/1-2 tbsps lime juice
Desiccated coconut

Dice the sweet potatoes and slice the chili pepper thinly. Mix together with the onion, garlic, ginger, cumin, coriander and allspice, coconut cream and water. Bring to the boil in a heavy-based saucepan and then simmer, uncovered, until the potato is almost tender. Add the shrimps, chicory, Chinese leaves/cabbage and a pinch of salt. Cook 4-5 minutes more until all the ingredients are hot but the leaves are still crisp. Add the sugar and lime juice to taste, if desired, before serving. Sprinkle with desiccated coconut.

## Trout with Chive Sauce

| | |
|---|---|
| **PREPARATION TIME:** 15 minutes | |
| **COOKING TIME:** 5-20 minutes | |
| **OVEN TEMPERATURE:** 400°F/ 200°C/Gas Mark 6 | |
| **SERVES:** 4 people | |

4 even-sized rainbow trout, gutted and
    fins trimmed
Flour mixed with salt and pepper for
    dredging
60ml/4 tbsps butter, melted
30ml/2 tbsps white wine
280ml/½ pint/1 cup double/heavy
    cream
1 small bunch chives, snipped
Salt and pepper

Dredge the trout with the seasoned flour and place on a lightly greased baking sheet. Spoon the melted butter over the fish. Bake in a 400°F/ 200°C/Gas Mark 6 oven for about 10 minutes, basting frequently with the butter. Cook until the skin is crisp. Check the fish on the underside close to the bone. If the fish is not cooked through, lower the oven temperature to 325°F/170°C/ Gas Mark 3 for a further 5 minutes.

Mix the dill, mustard and lemon juice or white wine together well. Cut three slits just through the skin on the sides of each fish. Spread half of the mustard mixture over each fish, pushing some of the mixture into each cut. Spoon over some of the melted butter and grill/broil the fish on one side for 5-6 minutes. Turn the fish over and spread the remaining mustard dill mixture onto the fish and spoon over the remaining melted butter. Grill/broil a further 5-6 minutes, or until the fish is cooked. Sprinkle the fish with salt and pepper before serving and arrange on a serving dish with the fresh dill and lemon wedges.

## Caribbean Shrimp and Sweet Potatoes in Coconut Sauce

| | |
|---|---|
| **PREPARATION TIME:** 20 minutes | |
| **COOKING TIME:** 20-30 minutes | |
| **SERVES:** 6 people | |

450g/1lb sweet potatoes, peeled
1 large onion, chopped
1 clove garlic, crushed
Small piece fresh ginger, grated
1 green or red chili pepper, de-seeded
1.25ml/¼ tsp cumin
1.25ml/¼ tsp coriander
1.25ml/¼ tsp allspice

Pour the wine into a small saucepan and bring to the boil. Boil to reduce by half. Pour on the cream and bring back to the boil. Allow to boil rapidly until the cream thickens slightly. Stir in the snipped chives, reserving some to sprinkle on top, if desired. When the fish are browned remove to a serving dish and spoon over some of the sauce. Sprinkle with the reserved chives and serve the rest of the sauce separately.

## Red Mullet with Herbs en Papillote

**PREPARATION TIME:** 20 minutes

**COOKING TIME:** 20-25 minutes

**OVEN TEMPERATURE:** 350°F/ 180°C/Gas Mark 4

**SERVES:** 4 people

*Oil*
*4 red mullet, gutted and trimmed*
*60g/4 tbsps butter*
*3 shallots, finely chopped*
*60ml/4 tbsps chopped herbs such as chervil, tarragon, marjoram, basil and parsley*
*60ml/4 tbsps dry white wine*
*Salt and pepper*

**GARNISH**
*Lemon wedges or slices*

Cut 4 circles of foil or greaseproof/ wax paper large enough to enclose each fish. Brush with oil and place 1 fish on half of each piece of foil or paper. Melt the butter and cook the shallots to brown lightly. Allow to cool slightly and add the herbs, salt

**Facing page: Trout with Chive Sauce. This page: Caribbean Shrimp and Sweet Potatoes in Coconut Sauce.**

and pepper. Pour 15ml/1 tbsp wine over each fish. Spoon the butter mixture on each fish and fold the other half of the paper or foil over the fish and seal the ends. Place the parcels in a roasting pan or on a baking sheet with a lip around the edge in case the parcels leak. Cook in a moderate oven for about 20-25 minutes, depending upon the size of the fish. Place the parcels on individual serving plates and allow each person to open their own just before ready to eat so that none of the flavour is lost. Serve with lemon wedges.

# HERBS AND SPICES

# RICE, PASTA, CHEESE AND EGGS

## Spaghetti alla Genovese

**PREPARATION TIME:** 10 minutes

**COOKING TIME:** 10 minutes

**SERVES:** 4 people

450g/1lb freshly cooked spaghetti
30g/2oz fresh basil leaves
15g/1oz fresh parsley
1 clove garlic, crushed
60g/4 tbsps pine nuts or chopped walnuts
60g/2oz/½ cup grated Parmesan cheese
140ml/¼ pint/½ cup olive oil
Salt and pepper

Combine basil, parsley, garlic, nuts, cheese, salt and pepper in a food processor or blender and work until finely chopped. With the machine running, pour the oil through the funnel in a thin, steady stream. Process until smooth and the consistency of mayonnaise. Pour over the pasta and toss to serve. Serve with additional grated cheese if desired.

## Noodles in Curry Sauce

**PREPARATION TIME:** 15 minutes

**COOKING TIME:** 20 minutes

**SERVES:** 4 people

450g/1lb thin egg noodles
30g/2 tbsps butter or margarine
1 medium-sized onion, finely chopped
1 clove garlic, crushed
10ml/2 tsps ground coriander
5ml/1 tsp ground fenugreek
5ml/1 tsp ground cumin
5ml/1 tsp ground turmeric
Pinch cayenne pepper
1-2 bananas, peeled and sliced
Juice of ½ lime

280ml/½ pint/1 cup stock
280ml/½ pint/1 cup whole milk yogurt
10ml/2 tsps chopped mint
Salt and pepper

Cook the noodles in boiling salted water until tender. Rinse under hot water and leave to drain. Melt butter or margarine in a large saucepan. Cook the onion to soften and add

**This page: Chive Crêpes with Cottage Cheese and Caviar. Facing page: Spaghetti alla Genovese (top), and Noodles in Curry Sauce (bottom).**

the garlic and spices. Cook 1 minute and add the bananas and lime juice. Cook to soften the bananas slightly, mashing with a fork. Pour on the

stock, cover and cook 20 minutes. Blend in the food processor or blender until smooth. Return to the rinsed-out pan and bring back to the boil. Take off the heat and add the yogurt, mint, salt and pepper. Pour the sauce over the noodles and toss before serving.

## Herb and Saffron Risotto with Peppers

**PREPARATION TIME:** 15 minutes

**COOKING TIME:** 30 minutes

**SERVES:** 4 people

45ml/3 tbsps olive oil
1 small onion, sliced
225g/8oz/1 cup Italian rissoto rice
Pinch saffron
1 bay leaf
5ml/1 tsp chopped fresh oregano
5ml/1 tsp chopped thyme leaves
5ml/1 tsp chopped basil or marjoram
10ml/2 tsps chopped flat parsley
Salt and pepper
750ml/1¼ pints/3 cups chicken or
    vegetable stock
1 small red pepper, sliced
1 small green pepper, sliced
60g/2oz/¼ cup grated fresh Parmesan
    cheese

Heat oil in a sauté pan. Add the onion and cook to soften. Add rice and cook until just opaque. Add saffron, bay leaf and herbs. Pour on stock and add salt and pepper. Stir well and cover the pan. Cook slowly about 15 minutes. Add the peppers, cover and cook a further 15 minutes, stirring occasionally until the rice is tender. Remove the bay leaf and stir in the cheese just before serving.

## Pasta with Sorrel and Cheese Sauce

**PREPARATION TIME:** 20 minutes

**COOKING TIME:** 12 minutes

**SERVES:** 4 people

450g/1lb freshly cooked pasta
120g/4oz sorrel
280ml/½ pint/1 cup chicken or vegetable
    stock

15ml/1 tbsp butter or margarine
15ml/ 1 tbsp flour
120ml/4 fl oz/½ cup heavy/double
    cream
60g/2oz/½ cup grated mild cheese
Salt and pepper
Pinch cayenne pepper
2 hard-boiled eggs, roughly chopped
Grated Parmesan cheese

Discard any thick stems of the sorrel. Cook the leaves in the stock for 4 minutes. Melt the butter and stir in the flour in a medium saucepan. Purée the sorrel in its stock in a blender or food processor and pour into the saucepan. Bring to the boil, stirring constantly. When thickened, stir in cream, salt, grated mild cheese, pepper, cayenne pepper and carefully stir in the eggs. Heat the sauce through gently. Pour over pasta and toss with Parmesan cheese to serve.

## Poached Eggs in Emerald Sauce

**PREPARATION TIME:** 20 minutes

**COOKING TIME:** 10 minutes

**SERVES:** 4 people

**DRESSING**
45ml/3 tbsps olive oil
15ml/1 tbsp lemon juice
5ml/1 tsp dill seed
Salt and pepper

120g/4oz mushrooms, quartered if large
450g/1lb spinach, well washed, thick
    stems removed
1 bunch watercress, thick stems trimmed
30ml/4 tbsps mixed, chopped fresh herbs
Pinch nutmeg
Pinch cayenne pepper
Salt and pepper
140ml/¼ pint/½ cup single/light cream
140ml/¼ pint/½ cup sour cream or
    yogurt
Salt and pepper
4 eggs, poached

**GARNISH**
Whole fresh herbs

Mix dressing and pour over mushrooms in a bowl. Refrigerate for

1 hour. Cook spinach 4 minutes in a covered saucepan in the water that clings to the leaves. Drain and reserve liquid. Purée with watercress and herbs until smooth, adding some of the spinach liquid. Add nutmeg, salt, pepper and a pinch cayenne pepper. Allow to cool completely. Stir in the cream and sour cream or yogurt. Meanwhile, poach 4 eggs in simmering water until the whites are just set but the yolks are still soft. A drop of vinegar or a pinch of salt in the water will help to set the whites. Drain the eggs and keep covered in cold water. Arrange on 4 serving plates. Garnish with herbs if desired and serve cold as a light main course or as a starter/appetizer.

## Pilau Rice

**PREPARATION TIME:** 30 minutes

**COOKING TIME:** 20 minutes

**SERVES:** 4 people

225g/8oz/1 cup basmati rice or long
    grain rice
30ml/2 tbsps oil
1 onion, finely chopped
10ml/2 tsps cassia bark
3 cloves
1 bay leaf, crumbled if dry, or snipped into
    thin strips if fresh
4 crushed green cardamom pods
570ml/1 pint/2 cups water or stock
Salt and pepper
60g/2oz/½ cup roasted, unsalted
    cashews
60g/2oz/½ cup raisins

Wash rice until the water runs almost clear. Leave to drain for 30 minutes. Heat oil and cook onion until soft but not coloured. Add the rice, cassia bark, cloves bay leaf and cardamom. Stir over moderate heat 2 minutes or until the rice begins to look opaque. Add salt and pepper and pour on the water or stock. Cover the pan tightly and cook over low heat for 10 minutes. Add the cashews and raisins and more liquid if the rice is dry. Cook, covered, a further 10 minutes or until the rice is tender and the liquid absorbed. Fluff with a fork before serving.

the rice in boiling salted water about 12 minutes or until tender. Drain, rinse under hot water and leave to dry. Cook two eggs for 10 minutes to hard boil. Melt the butter in a small pan and cook curry powder for 1 minute. Stir in 140ml/¼ pint/½ cup of the cooking liquid for the fish. Add cayenne pepper and cream. Flake the fish and mix with the rice. Chop the hard-boiled egg roughly and add to the rice and the fish. Add salt to taste and lemon or lime juice. Add the curry cream mixture and stir carefully. Put kedgeree into an oven-proof dish, cover loosely and heat through at 325°F/170°C/Gas Mark 3 for 15 minutes. Sprinkle on paprika and parsley to serve.

## Chive Crêpes with Cottage Cheese and Caviar

**PREPARATION TIME:** 30 minutes

**COOKING TIME:** 20 minutes

**SERVES:** 4-5 people

*120g/4oz/1 cup plain/all-purpose flour*
*Salt*
*1 egg*
*15ml/1 tbsp oil, melted butter or*
*   margarine*
*280ml/½ pint/1 cup milk*
*60ml/4 tbsps snipped chives*
*Pinch cayenne pepper*
*Oil for frying*

**FILLING**
*450g/1lb small curd cottage cheese*
*Salt and pepper*
*30ml/2 tbsps chopped parsley*

**TOPPING**
*60g/4 tbsps melted butter*
*Red or black caviar*

Sift the flour with a pinch of salt into a deep bowl. Make a well in the centre of the flour and break an egg into the well. Add the oil and pour in half the milk. Begin beating, gradually drawing in the flour from the sides. Alternatively, combine the flour, salt, egg, oil and milk in a food processor or blender. Process until smooth. Stir in the chives and cayenne pepper.

## Kedgeree

**PREPARATION TIME:** 15 minutes

**COOKING TIME:** 30 minutes

**SERVES:** 4-6 people

*225g/8oz smoked haddock or cod*
*Milk and water to cover fish*
*225g/8oz/1 cup long grain rice*
*1 bay leaf*
*2 hard-boiled eggs*
*10ml/2 tsps butter*
*15ml/1 tbsp mild curry powder*
*Pinch cayenne pepper*
*140ml/¼ pint/½ cup double/heavy*
*   cream*

**This page: Pasta with Sorrel and Cheese Sauce (top), and Poached Eggs in Emerald Sauce (bottom).**

*15ml/1 tbsp lime or lemon juice*
*30ml/2 tbsps chopped parsley*
*Salt*
*Paprika*

Place fish in a large pan, skin side up, and pour over enough milk and water mixed to cover the fish. Add the bay leaf, cover the pan and bring to the boil. Turn off the heat and leave to stand, covered tightly, for 15 minutes. The fish should cook in the heat of the liquid. Meanwhile, cook

Allow the batter to stand for 30 minutes before using. Add more milk if the batter thickens too much on standing. It should be the consistency of whipping cream. Brush a small amount of oil on a frying pan or crêpe pan and place the pan over high heat. When hot, pour in a large spoonful of batter. Quickly tilt the pan to cover the bottom evenly with the batter. Cook over a moderate heat until the edges are lightly browned. Lift with a palette knife/spatula and turn the crêpe over. Cook the other side and stack the crêpes on a plate and keep covered while cooking the others. The batter makes about 8 to 10 crêpes. Mix filling ingredients and spread on each crêpe. Roll up or fold in triangles and

**This page: Herb and Saffron Risotto with Peppers. Facing page: Pilau Rice (top), and Kedgeree (bottom).**

place in an oven-proof dish. Drizzle over the melted butter, cover and heat through at 325°F/170°C/Gas Mark 3 for 15 minutes. Top with caviar and serve.

# VEGETABLES, SALADS, OILS AND VINEGAR

## Broad Beans Provençal

**PREPARATION TIME:** 5 minutes

**COOKING TIME:** 8 minutes

**SERVES:** 4 people

450g/1lb fresh or frozen broad/lima beans
30g/2 tbsps butter
10ml/2 tsps Herbes de Provence
4 tomatoes, peeled, seeded and diced
Salt and pepper

Cook the broad/lima beans in boiling salted water until tender, about 8 minutes. Drain and refresh under cold water. Peel off outer skin if desired. Melt butter and toss with the broad beans and Herbes de Provence. Heat through and add tomatoes, salt and pepper. Serve immediately.

## Cucumbers with Dill Sauce

**PREPARATION TIME:** 15 minutes

**COOKING TIME:** 5 minutes

**SERVES:** 4 people

1 large cucumber, peeled in strips
180ml/6 fl oz/¾ cup double/heavy cream
10ml/2 tsps dill seed
10ml/2 tsps chopped fresh dill
10ml/2 tsps pink berries, drained if canned
Salt

Cut the cucumber in quarters, lengthwise. Remove the seeds and cut each quarter into 5cm/2 inch pieces. Cook in boiling salted water for 2 minutes, drain and refresh under cold water. Leave to drain completely. When the cucumbers are dry, combine the cream and dill seed in a small saucepan and bring to the boil. Allow to cook rapidly to thicken slightly. Strain and stir in the chopped dill, pink berries and a pinch of salt. Combine with

This page: **Mangetout/Pea Pods and Cauliflower with Ginger and Lemon Grass.** Facing page: **Cucumbers with Dill Sauce (top), and Broad Beans Provençal. (bottom).**

cucumbers. Serve immediately and do not reheat.

into each bottle. Seal and shake gently to mix. Leave for 2 weeks before using.

## Mangetout/Pea Pods and Cauliflower with Ginger and Lemon Grass

**PREPARATION TIME:** 20 minutes

**COOKING TIME:** 2 minutes

**SERVES:** 4-6 people

1 head cauliflower, broken into very small flowerets
225g/8oz mangetout/pea pods, ends trimmed
45ml/3 tbsps oil
10ml/2 tsps lemon juice
Pinch sugar
Salt and pepper
1 piece lemon grass, peeled and thinly sliced
1 small piece ginger, finely chopped
15ml/1 tbsp chopped parsley

Cook cauliflower in boiling salted water for 1 minute. Add the mangetout/pea pods and cook further 1 minute. Drain and refresh under cold water. Leave to drain dry. Mix the dressing ingredients together and add the ginger. Peel the outer layers from the lemon grass and use just the inner core. Slice thinly or chop finely. Mix with the dressing. Add the parsley to the dressing and pour over the vegetables, tossing to coat well. Serve cold.

## Tarragon and Lemon Vinegar

**PREPARATION TIME:** 10 minutes

**COOKING TIME:** 5 minutes

**MAKES:** 570ml/1 pint/2 cups

570ml/1 pint/2 cups white wine vinegar
Whole sprigs of tarragon, washed and dried
Peel of 1 lemon

Heat half the vinegar to boiling point. Add the tarragon and lemon peel. Leave to cool and mix with remaining vinegar. Bottle, placing 1 tarragon sprig and a piece of lemon peel in each bottle. Seal tightly and leave for 2 weeks before using.

**This page: Tomatoes with Orange and Tarragon. Facing page: Sherry Pepper Vinegar (left), and Tarragon and Lemon Vinegar (right).**

## Sherry Pepper Vinegar

**PREPARATION TIME:** 10 minutes

**COOKING TIME:** 5 minutes

**MAKES:** 430ml/¾ pint/1½ cups

280ml/½ pint/1 cup white wine vinegar
140ml/¼ pint/½ cup sherry
1 small dried red pepper per bottle

Warm the vinegar over gentle heat. Pour over the pepper in each bottle. Allow to cool and pour the sherry

## Tomatoes with Orange and Tarragon

**PREPARATION TIME:** 20 minutes

**COOKING TIME:** 10 minutes

**SERVES:** 4 people

450g/1lb cherry tomatoes or 8 small tomatoes
Zest and juice of 1 orange
10ml/2 tsps chopped fresh tarragon
5ml/1 tsp lemon juice
2.5ml/½ tsp sugar
15ml/1 tbsp oil
Salt and pepper

140ml/¼ pint/½ cup crème fraiche (thick
  soured cream)

**GARNISH**
Small tarragon sprigs or whole leaves

Place the tomatoes in a bowl and
pour over boiling water to cover.
Leave 20 seconds, drain and put
immediately into cold water. Peel and
remove the cores. Remove the zest
from the orange in thin strips and set
aside. Squeeze the juice and measure
out 30ml/2 tbsps and combine with
tarragon, lemon juice, sugar, oil, salt
and pepper and whisk well.
Gradually add the crème fraiche.
Do not over whisk once the crème is
added. If the sauce is too thick, add
orange juice to thin slightly. Pour
over the tomatoes and garnish with
sprigs of tarragon or whole leaves
and reserved orange zest. Serve
chilled.

## Spiced Cauliflower

| | |
|---|---|
| **PREPARATION TIME:** 20 minutes | |
| **COOKING TIME:** 20 minutes | |
| **SERVES:** 4 people | |

1 large cauliflower, washed and trimmed

**SAUCE**
15g/1 tbsp butter or margarine
15g/1 tbsp flour
2.5ml/½ tsp dry mustard
1.25ml/¼ tsp nutmeg
280ml/½ pint/1 cup milk
Pinch mace
Salt and pepper
45g/3 tbsps grated sharp cheese
Additional nutmeg

Place whole cauliflower in boiling
salted water and cook, uncovered, for
about 15 minutes. Drain well and
keep warm. Melt the butter or
margarine for the sauce and stir in
the flour off the heat. Stir in the dry
mustard and nutmeg and gradually
add the milk. Add the pinch of mace
and salt and pepper. Bring to the boil,
stirring constantly until thick. Add
the cheese and stir to melt. Coat the
cauliflower with the sauce and
sprinkle with additional nutmeg.

Brown under a grill/broiler, if
desired.
*Recipe courtesy Schwartz Spices Limited*

## Sunshine Carrots

| | |
|---|---|
| **PREPARATION TIME:** 15 minutes | |
| **COOKING TIME:** 15-20 minutes | |
| **SERVES:** 4 people | |

450g/1lb carrots, peeled and sliced
5ml/1 tsp light brown sugar
5ml/1 tsp cornflour/cornstarch
1.25ml/¼ tsp salt
1.25ml/¼ tsp ground ginger
140ml/¼ pint/½ cup unsweetened
  orange juice
30g/2 tbsps butter
Fresh ginger, peeled and shredded

Place the carrots in cold, salted water,
cover and bring to the boil. Cook
about 15 minutes, drain well and
keep warm. Combine all the
remaining ingredients except the
fresh ginger and butter in a small
saucepan. Bring to the boil, stirring
constantly until thickened. Beat in
the butter and pour over the carrot
in a serving dish. Sprinkle with the
shredded fresh ginger.
*Recipe courtesy Schwartz Spices Limited*

## Marjoram Potatoes and Onions

| | |
|---|---|
| **PREPARATION TIME:** 15 minutes | |
| **COOKING TIME:** 40 minutes | |
| **OVEN TEMPERATURE:** 350°F/ 180°C/Gas Mark 4 | |
| **SERVES:** 4 people | |

4 medium potatoes, peeled and sliced
  thickly
4 medium onions, sliced
10ml/2 tsps marjoram, chopped
Salt and pepper
Butter

Layer the potatoes and onions in an
ovenproof dish or a piece of foil for

**Facing page: New Potatoes with
Bel Paese and Summer Savory
(top), and Marjoram Potatoes and
Onions (bottom).**

barbecueing. Sprinkle with marjoram, salt and pepper and dot with butter. Bake in a moderate oven for 40 minutes. Alternatively, cook over hot coals on a barbecue for 30-40 minutes.
*Recipe courtesy Schwartz Spices Limited*

## Spiced Oil

| | |
|---|---|
| **PREPARATION TIME:** | 10 minutes |
| **COOKING TIME:** | 5 minutes |
| **MAKES:** | 570ml/1 pint/2 cups |

*570ml/1 pint/2 cups light vegetable oil*
*3 cloves*
*3 whole allspice berries*
*1 cinnamon stick*
*15ml/1 tbsp coriander seeds*
*4 cardamom pods, crushed*
*12 whole black peppercorns*
*Peel of ½ an orange*

Warm the oil in a saucepan over gentle heat, pour over the spices and allow to cool. Pour into bottles, including some of the spices and a piece of orange rind, and seal each bottle tightly. Keep for 2 weeks before using.

## New Potatoes with Bel Paese and Summer Savory

| | |
|---|---|
| **PREPARATION TIME:** | 20 minutes |
| **COOKING TIME:** | 20 minutes |
| **SERVES:** | 4-6 people |

*900g/2lbs new or small red potatoes, scrubbed but not peeled*
*180g/6oz Bel Paese cheese*
*60-90ml/4-6 tbsps milk or single/light cream*
*Salt and pepper*
*Summer savory, chopped*

Cook potatoes in salted water 20 minutes or until tender. Drain and cut in half if potatoes are large. Leave small potatoes whole. Mix the cheese and milk or cream together. Add more milk or cream if the cheese is still too thick. Mix in salt and pepper and add the potatoes, stirring to coat. Sprinkle on the summer savory and serve immediately. Do not reheat.

## Herb and Garlic Oil

| | |
|---|---|
| **PREPARATION TIME:** | 10 minutes |
| **COOKING TIME:** | 5 minutes |
| **MAKES:** | 570ml/1 pint/2 cups |

*570ml/1 pint/2 cups light vegetable oil and olive oil mixed half and half*
*Fresh whole herbs*
*A sliver of garlic*
*Juniper berries*

**This page: Sunshine Carrots (top), and Spiced Cauliflower (bottom). Facing page: Spiced Oil (left), and Herb and Garlic Oil (right).**

Pour the oil into bottles and wash and dry the herbs and push equal amounts of herbs into each bottle. Put a sliver of garlic and a few juniper berries into each bottle. Seal tightly and keep 2 weeks before using.

# HERBS AND SPICES

# DESSERTS, PRESERVES AND BAKING

## Spiced Cream Cake

| | |
|---|---|
| **PREPARATION TIME:** 15 minutes | |
| **COOKING TIME:** 25 minutes | |
| **OVEN TEMPERATURE:** 350°F/ 180°C/Gas Mark 4 | |
| **MAKES:** 1 Cake | |

225g/8oz/1 cup butter or margarine
450g/1lb/2 cups light brown sugar
4 eggs
360g/12oz/3 cups plain/all-purpose
    flour, sifted
25ml/1½ tbsps baking powder
7.5ml/1½ tsps ground cinnamon
2.5ml/½ tsp ground nutmeg
2.5ml/½ tsp ground allspice
1.25ml/¼ tsp ground cloves
Salt
240ml/8 fl oz/1 cup milk

**FILLING**
280ml/½ pint/1 cup cream, whipped
    with 15ml/1 tbsp sugar
60ml/4 tbsps thick sour cream or natural
    yogurt
Cyrstalized carrots

Pre-heat the oven and grease 3 20cm/8 inch round cake pans and line the bases with circles of greaseproof/waxed paper. Cream the butter and sugar together until light and fluffy. Beat in the eggs 1 at a time, beating well in-between each addition. Sift the flour with the baking powder, spices, and salt. Gradually add the flour mixture to the butter, sugar and eggs and beat just until smooth. Stir in the milk by hand. Divide among the three prepared cake pans and bake in a moderate oven for about 25 minutes or until the cake springs back when touched lightly with a fingertip. Cool the cake in the pans on a rack for a few minutes and then loosen the cake from the sides of the pan and turn out onto the rack to

**This page: Spiced Cream Cake.
Facing page: Spiced Crème Brûlée.**

and slowly bring to the boil, stirring occasionally. Allow the syrup to boil about 2 minutes to thicken slightly. Pour the syrup over the apples. Serve warm or cold with whipped cream.

## Oranges in Mint Sauce

**PREPARATION TIME:** 20 minutes

**COOKING TIME:** 5 minutes

**SERVES:** 4 people

280ml/½ pint/1 cup honey
430ml/¾ pint/1½ cups water
2 large sprigs mint
12 whole cloves
4 oranges

**GARNISH**
4 sprigs mint

Combine honey and water in a heavy saucepan. Add the mint and cloves and bring slowly to the boil. Stir to dissolve the honey. Allow to boil rapidly for 5 minutes or until syrupy. Cool completely. Remove the mint and cloves. Remove peel from 1 orange with a zester and set it aside. Alternatively, peel the orange, scrape the white pith from the peel and cut the peel into very fine strips. Put the strips into the syrup. Peel the oranges, completely removing the pith. Slice thinly into rounds, but do not cut completely through the orange. Pour over the syrup. Sprinkle over the strips of orange zest if not added to the syrup. Garnish with sprigs of fresh mint.

cool. Spread the bottom layer with some of the crystalized carrot and then top with half of the cream. Repeat with the second layer and top with third layer. Dredge the top with icing/powdered sugar.

## Spiced Apples with Summer Savory

**PREPARATION TIME:** 15 minutes

**COOKING TIME:** 15 minutes

**SERVES:** 4 people

675g/1½ lbs dessert apples or apples that
   hold their shape when cooked
1 cinnamon stick
3 whole cloves
Sugar to taste
Water to cover

**This page: Spiced Tapioca. Facing page: Oranges in Mint Sauce (top), and Spiced Apples with Summer Savory (bottom).**

10ml/2 tsps chopped summer savory
60ml/4 tbsps white wine
Whipped cream to serve

Peel, core and thickly slice the apples. Put them into a heavy pan with the sugar, spices and enough water to just cover them. Cook slowly, covered, until the apples are soft and slightly translucent. Do not allow the apples to boil or they will break apart. When the apples are cooked remove them to a serving dish, remove the cinnamon and cloves from the syrup and discard. Add the chopped summer savory and wine to the syrup

## Spiced Tapioca

**PREPARATION TIME:** 30 minutes

**COOKING TIME:** 20 minutes

**SERVES:** 4-6 people

60g/2oz/¼ cup tapioca
570ml/1 pint/2 cups milk
1 vanilla pod
30g/2 tbsps sugar
8 small cardamoms, seeds removed and
   crushed
280ml/½ pint/1 cup whipping cream
12 ratafias
Pistachio nuts

Combine the tapioca, milk, vanilla pod, sugar and cardamom seeds in a heavy saucepan and cook until the tapioca softens and swells in size. Pour the tapioca into a bowl and remove the vanilla pod. Leave to cool completely. Cover the top of the tapioca with a sheet of clingfilm/plastic wrap to prevent a skin from forming. Whip the cream lightly. Remove the clingfilm/plastic wrap when the tapioca is completely cool and fold in the cream. Spoon the tapioca into a large glass bowl or individual serving dishes. Crush the ratafias coarsely and chop the pistachio nuts. Sprinkle the ratafias and pistachio nuts on top of the tapioca pudding to serve.

## Rasmalai

**PREPARATION TIME:** 15 minutes, plus overnight to drain

**COOKING TIME:** 30 minutes

**SERVES:** 4 people

1¾ litres/3 pints/6 cups milk
Lemon juice
10ml/2 tsps plain/all-purpose flour
8 green cardamoms, crushed
2-3 sugar cubes, cut in 12 small pieces

**MILK SAUCE**
570ml/1 pint/2 cups milk, reduced by
    boiling to 430ml/¾ pint/1½ cups

**SYRUP**
350g/12oz/1½ cups granulated sugar
280ml/½ pint/1 cup water

**GARNISH**
Few drops rosewater or orange flower
    water
30g/2 tbsps pistachio nuts, chopped
30g/2 tbsps almonds, chopped

Bring the 1¾ litre/3 pints/6 cups of milk to the boil and add lemon juice. Leave to stand to separate. Cool for 10 minutes and then strain through a fine sieve or a clean piece of muslin/cheesecloth. Leave to drain overnight. Boil the milk to reduce it and prepare the sugar syrup. Combine the granulated sugar and water in a saucepan and cook for 2-3 minutes to dissolve the sugar. Turn

up the heat and allow to boil for about 3 minutes or until syrupy. Transfer the drained milk mixture to a bowl and beat with an electric mixer or wooden spoon for about 5 minutes to soften. Add the flour and the cardamom seeds gradually, and continue mashing. Set aside for 2-3 minutes. Divide the mixture into 12 equal-sized balls. Place a piece of sugar cube in the centre of each ball and then press gently to flatten it into a 4cm/1½ inch round. Continue until all the milk mixture is drained. Bring the sugar syrup back to simmering point and drop in the rasmalai balls, a few at a time. Allow them to boil for 10 minutes. Transfer the milk sauce to a serving dish. Remove the rasmalai from the syrup and place in the milk sauce. When all the rasmalai are cooked and in the milk sauce, sprinkle with rose or orange flower water and the chopped nuts. Allow to cool and refrigerate before serving.

## Spiced Crème Brûlée

**PREPARATION TIME:** 15 minutes

**COOKING TIME:** 20 minutes

**SERVES:** 4 people

280ml/½ pint/1 cup milk
280ml/½ pint/1 cup double/heavy
    cream
1 stick cinnamon
10ml/2 tsps coriander seed, slightly
    crushed
1 vanilla pod
4 egg yolks
25ml/1½ tbsps cornflour/cornstarch
90g/3oz/⅓ cup sugar
Demerara or light brown sugar

Pour the milk into a heavy-based saucepan and add the spices and vanilla pod. Heat gently. Beat the egg yolks, cornflour and sugar together until light. Bring the milk and cream just to boiling point and strain onto the egg yolk mixture, pouring gradually and beating constantly. Return the custard to the rinsed-out pan and place over gentle heat. Bring the mixture to the boil, stirring constantly with a wooden spoon. When the mixture coats the back of

the spoon remove from the heat. Do not allow to boil rapidly. Strain into 4 ramekin dishes/custard cups. The custard should come almost to the top. Chill until set. Put the custards into a roasting pan and surround with ice. Pre-heat a grill/broiler to the highest temperature. Sprinkle a thin layer of the sugar over the top of each custard and put under the heat. Rotate the cups and move the pan around until the sugar melts and caramelizes. Chill until the sugar layer is hard and crisp. Serve with biscuits/cookies or fruit.

## Spiced Banana Fritters

**PREPARATION TIME:** 15 minutes

**COOKING TIME:** 20 minutes

**SERVES:** 4-6 people

6 very ripe bananas
2 eggs, separated
2.5ml/½ tsp ground nutmeg
2.5ml/½ tsp ground ginger
60g/2oz/¼ cup plain/all-purpose flour
Oil for shallow frying
60ml/4 tbsps dark rum (optional)
60g/4 tbsps sugar
10ml/2 tsps ground cinnamon

Peel the bananas and slice into large pieces. Place in a bowl with the egg yolks, nutmeg and ginger. Beat with an electric mixer until well mixed but not completely smooth. Pour in enough flour to make a thick mixture. Beat the egg whites until stiff but not dry and fold into the banana mixture. Heat the oil in a large frying pan and drop in the banana mixture by spoonfuls. Fry the fritters until golden brown on both sides. Arrange on a serving plate and drizzle over the rum, if using. Mix the sugar and cinnamon together and sprinkle over the fritters before serving. Serve hot with cream if desired.

**Facing page: Spiced Banana Fritters (top), and Rasmalai (bottom).**

## Spiced Damson Cheese

**PREPARATION TIME:** 15 minutes

**COOKING TIME:** 1-1¼ hours

**MAKES:** Approximately 450g/1lb/
2 cups

675g/1½ lbs damsons or small purple
  plums
900g/2lbs/4 cups granulated sugar
Water
1 bay leaf
4 whole cloves
1 small piece stick cinnamon

Wash the fruit and remove stems and
leaves. Put the fruit into a deep,
heavy-based pan and add water to
half-cover the fruit. Simmer the fruit
gently until thoroughly soft. Rub
through a strainer. Do not use a food
processor or blender. Weigh or
measure the pulp and allow 450g/
1lb/2 cups sugar to every 450g/1lb/
2 cups of pulp. Combine the pulp
and sugar in the rinsed out pan.
Tie the bay leaf, cloves and
cinnamon in a muslin/cheesecloth
bag and add to the damsons. Bring to
the boil and allow to cook over
moderate heat for 1-1¼ hours, stirring
constantly. When the mixture is thick
remove the muslin/cheesecloth bag.
When the mixture is cold it should
be firm enough to slice. Set in a loaf
pan and allow to cool. Chill until
firm. May be served as a pudding/
dessert with cream. If a softer, more
spreadable mixture is desired, double
the quantity of water. Pour this
mixture into sterilized jars, seal and
keep in a cool place. Keep the
damson cheese refrigerated after
opening the jar.

## Crystalized Carrots

**PREPARATION TIME:** 10 minutes

**COOKING TIME:** 45 minutes

**MAKES:** 430ml/¾ pint/1½ cups

225g/8oz carrots, peeled and shredded
225g/8oz/1 cup granulated sugar
Zest and juice of 1 lemon
3 cardamom pods, slightly crushed
1 small piece ginger, peeled and left whole

Place the shredded carrot in a deep,
heavy-based pan and cover with
water. Bring to the boil and then
allow to simmer until tender. Stir in
the sugar and add the lemon zest and
juice, cardamom seeds and ginger.
Allow to simmer, stirring often. Bring
to the boil and allow to cook rapidly
just until the shreds of carrot are
glazed with sugar. Remove the ginger
and the cardamom seeds and spoon
the mixture into sterilized jars. Seal
and store in a cool place. Keep
refrigerated after opening.

**This page: Cranberry Snow with
Mint. Facing page: Spiced Damson
Cheese (top), and Crystalized
Carrots. (bottom).**

## Gingerbread

**PREPARATION TIME:** 15 minutes

**COOKING TIME:** 1 hour

**OVEN TEMPERATURE:** 325°F/
170°C/Gas Mark 3

**MAKES:** 1 Cake

120g/4oz/½ cup butter or margarine
120ml/4 fl oz/½ cup treacle or molasses
225g/8oz/1 cup light brown sugar
120ml/4 fl oz/½ cup hot water
300g/10oz/2¼ cups whole-wheat flour
10ml/2 tsps baking powder
Pinch salt
10ml/2 tsps fresh ginger, peeled and
    grated
5ml/1 tsp grated nutmeg
1 egg, beaten

Melt the butter in a heavy-based pan and stir in the molasses and sugar. Heat gently to dissolve molasses and sugar. Pour in the hot water, mix well and set the mixture aside. Sift the flour with the baking powder and salt into a large bowl. Return the bran from the flour to the bowl. Make a well in the centre and add the nutmeg, ginger and beaten egg. Pour in the molasses liquid and begin beating with a wooden spoon, gradually drawing in the flour from the outside. Alternatively, use an electric mixer, but be careful not to over mix. Line a shallow round or square pan with lightly greased paper. Bake in a pre-heated oven for 1 hour, or until a skewer inserted into the centre of the cake comes out clean. Serve with whipped or sour cream, or slice and spread with butter.

## Saffron Teacakes

**PREPARATION TIME:** 15 minutes

**COOKING TIME:** 20-30 minutes

**OVEN TEMPERATURE:** 350°F/
180°C/Gas Mark 4

140ml/¼ pint/½ cup milk
Pinch saffron
225g/8oz/2 cups self-raising flour or
    plain/all-purpose flour plus
    15ml/1 tbsp baking powder
120g/4oz/½ cup margarine or vegetable
    shortening
120g/4oz/1 cup currants
2.5ml/½ tsp allspice
30g/2 tbsps candied peel
60g/2oz/¼ cup sugar
Pinch salt
1 egg

Heat 60ml/4 tbsps of the milk and add saffron. Leave to stand 10-15 minutes. Sift the flour with the baking powder, if using. Cut the margarine or shortening into the flour with 2 knives, or use an electric mixer or food processor. Stir in the currants, allspice, candied peel and sugar. Combine saffron milk with the rest of the milk and add to the flour, mixing to form a soft dough. Roll the dough out in a circle 1.25cm/½ inch thick. Cut into rounds with a pastry cutter. Beat 1 egg with a pinch of salt and brush over the surface of the cakes to glaze. Bake in a moderate oven for 20-30 minutes. Split and spread with butter or serve with damson cheese.

## Cinnamon Coeur à la Crème with Rosehip Syrup

**PREPARATION TIME:** 15 minutes
**SERVES:** 4-6 people

225g/8oz cream cheese, softened
400ml/12 fl oz/1¼ cups whipping cream
90g/3oz/⅔ cup icing/powdered sugar,
    sifted
10ml/2 tsps ground cinnamon

Beat the cream cheese with an electric mixer until light and fluffy. Mix in 60ml/4 tbsps of the cream and beat until smooth. Mix in the sugar and the cinnamon. Whip the remaining cream to soft peaks and fold into the cream cheese mixture. Line 1 large Coeur à la Crème mould, or 4 to 6 individual moulds, with dampened muslin/cheesecloth, extending beyond the edges of the mould. Spoon in the cheese mixture and spread out evenly. Fold the overlapping ends of the muslin/cheesecloth over the top of the mixture and place the mould or moulds on a rack set over a pan. Refrigerate for at least 8 hours or overnight. Just before serving, unwrap the muslin/cheesecloth and invert the mould onto a plate. Carefully peel away all the cheesecloth. Pour over some of the prepared rosehip syrup and serve the rest separately. Decorate with rosettes of whipped cream and candied rose petals if desired.

## Cranberry Snow with Mint

**PREPARATION TIME:** 15 minutes

**SERVES:** 4 people

*60g/2oz/1 cup fresh or frozen cranberries*
*30g/2 tbsps granulated sugar*
*2 egg whites*
*60g/4 tbsps sugar*
*140ml/¼ pint/½ cup whipping cream*
*140ml/¼ pint/½ cup natural yogurt*
*30ml/2 tbsps chopped fresh mint*

**GARNISH**
*Whole sprigs fresh mint*

Combine the cranberries and 30g/2 tbsps of sugar in a small, heavy-based pan. Cook slowly until juice forms and the cranberries soften. Set aside to cool completely. When the cranberries are cool, whisk the egg whites until stiff but not dry. Gradually whisk in the 60g/4 tbsps sugar. Whisk well in between each addition of sugar until stiff peaks form and the egg whites are smooth and glossy. Whip the cream until thick, and combine with the yogurt. Fold the egg whites into the cream and yogurt mixture along with the cooled cranberries and the chopped mint. Do not over-fold, the mixture should look marbled. Spoon into

individual serving dishes and garnish with the whole sprigs of mint. Make and eat the same day.

## Rosehip Syrup

**PREPARATION TIME:** 15 minutes

**COOKING TIME:** 1½ hours

**MAKES:** 570ml/1 pint/2 cups

*900g/2lbs rosehips*
*1 stick cinnamon*
*1150ml/2 pints/4-5 cups water*
*340g/12oz/1½ cups sugar*
*Juice of 1 lemon*

Wash the rosehips well and chop them. Put into a large saucepan with

**Facing page: Gingerbread (top), and Saffron Teacakes (bottom). This page: Rosehip Syrup (top), and Cinnamon Coeur à la Crème with Rosehip Syrup (bottom).**

the cinnamon and water and cover. Cook very slowly for 1 hour or until soft. Stir frequently. Strain and make up or reduce to 570ml/1 pint/2 cups and stir in the sugar. Heat slowly to dissolve the sugar and then allow the mixture to boil until it becomes syrupy. Skim off scum from the surface as it forms. Add the lemon juice and pour into sterilized jars and seal.

# HERBS AND SPICES

Asparagus and Chervil Soup 10
Borscht 10
Broad Beans Provençal 46
Caribbean Shrimp and Sweet Potatoes in Coconut Sauce 38
Carrot and Basil Soup 8
Chicken Cacciatore 26
Chicken Liver Pâté with Coriander 28
Chicken Marrakesh with Peppers and Coriander 22
Chicken Moghlai with Coriander Chutney 25
Chicken Stew Niçoise 16
Chili with Three Beans 8
Chive Crêpes with Cottage Cheese and Caviar 43
Cinnamon Coeur à la Crème with Rosehip Syrup 62
Country Herb Pâté 16
Cranberry Snow with Mint 63
Crystalized Carrots 60
Cucumbers with Dill Sauce 46
Devilled Birds in Pasta Nests 14
Duck with Cranberries and Mangoes 19
Five Spice Pork 22
Fried Pheasant with Chestnuts and Tarragon 14
Ginger and Almond Meatballs 19
Gingerbread 60
Gravad Laks with Mustard Dill Sauce 34
Grilled/Broiled Herring with Dill and Mustard 36

Grilled/Broiled Pork Chops with Herbs and Pink Berries 20
Ham with Spiced Raisin Sauce 22
Herb and Garlic Oil 52
Herb and Saffron Risotto with Peppers 42
Herb-Roasted Guinea Fowl with Redcurrants 24
Kedgeree 43
Liver with Coriander Lemon and Pine Nuts 25
Mangetout/Pea Pods and Cauliflower with Ginger and Lemon Grass 48
Marjoram Potatoes and Onions 50
Mediterranean Lamb with Vegetables 18
Moroccan Chicken 22
Mussels in Ginger-Cumin Sauce 32
Navarin of Lamb Printanier 28
New Potatoes with Bel Paese and Summer Savory 52
Noodles in Curry Sauce 40
Oranges in Mint Sauce 56
Pasta with Sorrel and Cheese Sauce 42
Pea Soup with Mint 10
Pilau Rice 42
Poached Eggs in Emerald Sauce 42
Poached Smoked Haddock in Herb Sauce 36
Prawns/Shrimp with Red Pepper Sauce 34
Rasmalai 58

Red Mullet with Herbs en Papillote 39
Rosehip Syrup 63
Saffron Teacakes 62
Sauté Lamb with Fennel and Orange 20
Scallops in Saffron Sauce 32
Seviche 34
Sherry Pepper Vinegar 48
Spaghetti alla Genovese 40
Spiced Apples with Summer Savory 56
Spiced Banana Fritters 58
Spiced Cauliflower 50
Spiced Cream Cake 54
Spiced Crème Brûlée 58
Spiced Damson Cheese 60
Spiced Oil 52
Spiced Pâté with Peppercorns 16
Spiced Tapioca 56
Spinach and Chicken Terrine 28
Sunshine Carrots 50
Tarragon and Lemon Vinegar 48
Tomato and Tarragon Soup 8
Tomatoes with Orange and Tarragon 48
Trout with Chive Sauce 38
Tunisian Beef Stew with Okra 28
Veal with Mushrooms and Herbs 13
Veal with Sorrel and Cheese Filling 13